FUNERAL AND MEMORIAL SERVICE
READINGS, POEMS AND TRIBUTES

FUNERAL AND MEMORIAL SERVICE READINGS, POEMS AND TRIBUTES

Edited by
Rachel R. Baum

McFarland & Company, Inc., Publishers
Jefferson, North Carolina, and London

The present work is a reprint of the library bound edition of Funeral and Memorial Service Readings, Poems and Tributes, *first published in 1999 by McFarland.*

LIBRARY OF CONGRESS CATALOGUING-IN-PUBLICATION DATA

Funeral and memorial service readings, poems and tributes / edited by
   Rachel R. Baum.
      p.   cm.
   Includes bibliographical references (p.   ) and index.

   ISBN-13: 978-0-7864-3729-0
   softcover : 50# alkaline paper ∞

   1. Death—Literary collections.   2. Funeral rites and ceremonies—
Handbooks, manuals, etc.   3. Memorial rites and ceremonies—
Handbooks, manuals, etc.   4. Memorial services— Handbooks,
manuals, etc.   5. Funeral services—Handbooks, manuals, etc.
6. Bereavement—Literary collections.   7. Grief—Literary collections.
I. Baum, Rachel R., 1956–
PN6071.D4F86   2008
808.8'03548—dc21   99-29046

British Library cataloguing data are available

Cover photograph ©2008 Shutterstock

Manufactured in the United States of America

McFarland & Company, Inc., Publishers
   Box 611, Jefferson, North Carolina 28640
      www.mcfarlandpub.com

To Ariel and Sydney

and in memory of
Jerzy Kosinski

TABLE OF CONTENTS

ACKNOWLEDGMENTS

Every effort has been made to trace the ownership of copyrighted material. If any infringement has been made, I offer my apologies, and I will be happy, upon receiving notification, to make proper acknowledgments in future editions of this collection. I would like to take this opportunity to express gratitude to all authors and owners of copyrighted material for permissions generously extended. Thanks go to the Authors Registry, Inc., with special appreciation to Dick King for his patience, the Society of Authors in London, England, and to WATCH, a joint project of the Harry Ransom Humanities Research Center at the University of Texas at Austin and the University of Reading Library, Reading, England, for helping me track down elusive copyright owners.

My research consisted of reading any book of poetry I could get my hands on. Both bookstores and libraries have provided unending resources, but I would especially like to acknowledge the generosity of the member libraries of the Upper Hudson Library System, particularly the Bethlehem Public Library in Delmar, New York. The Internet is becoming a better finding tool, although electronic mail is a more productive one. The librarians of the Stumpers-L listserv and the resulting Stumpers archives have been a part of my daily email for several years, and an engaging source of potential poems. Some poets, on learning of this compilation, offered additional creations of their own for consideration. Many thanks to Leslie Fine and Shelby Forrest, and also to Yaedi Ignatow, who was warm and generous with her own poems and those of her father—she is his legacy.

Thanks to friends who have given me poems, advice or respite: Susan Birkhead, Laura Weissenberg, Nancy Gorham Haiman, Larry Baker, and Sheree Mirochnik. Thank you especially to my great and good friend, Julie Beth Todaro, for the sustenance I have come to depend on all these years. She is my working week and my Sunday rest.

I am grateful for the love of my parents, and for my sister, who is always proud of me and I of her.

I am thankful for my husband, children and dogs — for teasing me so I wouldn't take myself so seriously, for bringing me chamomile tea, for keeping my lap warm at night and for all their encouragement, enthusiasm and support for this project. They may now have the computer back.

Therefore all poems are elegies.
— George Barker

PREFACE

After the release of the film *Four Weddings and a Funeral*, libraries throughout the country were besieged by people requesting the text to "that poem" which was read at the funeral of one of the main characters. As many librarians discovered, traditional reference tools such as *Granger's Index to Poetry* could not help them locate the work, and the film was too new at the time to be cited in filmographies. The task was made even more difficult since the poem itself was not named in the movie. Ultimately, they would discover that it was the W.H. Auden poem known variously as "Stop the Clock," "Funeral Blues" and "Twelve Songs." This was not an isolated incident. The poem read at Denys Finch-Hatton's grave in the film *Out of Africa* had the same effect, as did the readings from the public funerals of *Challenger* space shuttle astronaut Christa McAuliffe and Princess Diana.

The bereaved often search for poems to read at the funeral or memorial service of a loved one. Words and creativity can fail even the most articulate and expressive person when confronted with the stress of having to speak at a loved one's funeral. Those responsible for eulogizing or paying tribute want to find something appropriate and meaningful to say. Yet since funerals are usually held within a few short days after the death, there is little time for the relative or friend to try to find something suitable at the library or bookstore. A recent *Town & Country* magazine article states, "Memorial services are a way for people to say good-bye to those who have died. The services used to be quite religious in nature, but now people have secular gatherings or incorporate religious ceremony with secular practice. Music, humor and personal touches are important for services." (Jim Brosseau, "In Memoriam." *Town & Country Monthly*, January 1996, v. 150 n. 5188 p. 38). While subject searches of *Granger's* can uncover many such works, no reference tool currently exists that collects, in one accessible resource, poems to meet those needs.

This book is a collection of poetry and prose appropriate for reading at a funeral or memorial service. To assist the user in finding a reading that meets his or her needs, the book is divided into eleven chapters, with tributes for mothers; fathers; children; husbands, wives and lovers; friends; men; women; sisters and brothers; soldiers; companion animals and pets; and a section of readings appropriate for any loved one. The book is indexed by author, by title, by first line, by the film or novel in which a work is cited, by the person at whose funeral or memorial service a poem was read, and by the person performing the recitation.

Although this book is not intended as a guide to funeral planning or grief counseling, I have appended a section of selected resources for before and after the funeral. I wanted to be sure that if this book is the only one that a grieving person picks up to prepare for an upcoming funeral, additional help was available if needed. The books cited in the Appendix should be available at your local public library or bookstore. Support organizations and bereavement Internet sites are listed as well.

When I was nine years old, I came across Christina Rossetti's poem *Remember*. Its words, cadence, and simple theme made an impact on my sensitive preadolescent nature. It became the first poem I ever cared enough to memorize on my own and the first in what would become a burgeoning collection. I cut it from the newspaper and saved it in my sock drawer. Gradually, a little pile of clippings grew from that first discovery and with it, a love of poetry. Over the years, I read anthologies, literary magazines, chapbooks and collections; famous and little known poets; and writers of fiction and prose who also happened to write a verse or two. For this book, I also used the Internet, which is a remarkable and frustrating tool. I found many poems from monitoring poetry listservs, various bulletin boards, and ever-changing web sites.

I looked primarily for readings that moved me. Most of these poems "read" well; that is, the words flow smoothly when spoken, and it would not be a stretch of the imagination to envision them being recited at a service. Poems of a spiritual nature were included also, provided that any references made to a higher being were nonsectarian. I also chose brief readings that seemed to sum up a person's life, or that captured the mourner's relationship with the deceased. It was particularly important to me to choose some tributes that would be acceptable for stillborn, aborted or miscarried children. Grief in any circumstance can be difficult to articulate. For a baby who has never lived, it is nearly impossible to express. I believe the few works I was able to locate have somehow conveyed awareness of that very personal experience.

The simplest way to use this book is to turn to the appropriate section and read or glance through the pieces until one in particular seems right. So, a person who had lost his sister would refer to Chapter Six: Those Who Walk with Me to find a poem such as *Goblin Market*. However, if none of the readings in Chapter Six meets his or her needs, the section on women (Chapter Ten: Woman Much Missed) or the general section (Chapter Eleven: I Cannot Forget You) might have something suitable. Each section has an introduction with ideas on other chapters that might contain the perfect poem.

To find a poem or a reading from a film, video or made-for-TV movie, look up the title of the movie in the index to films, novels, and famous persons beginning on page 163. This index also includes poems read at the funerals of some well-known people. It is a short, selective list, since many celebrity funeral and memorial services are private and the readings not made public.

A eulogy or a memorial tribute may be the most difficult speech anyone ever has to make. For that reason, the selection to be read should be one the person is comfortable reading aloud. Most people not only understand but are sympathetic and supportive if the reader must pause for composure or is even unable to complete the reading.

After identifying the appropriate poem, rewrite the selection in large type or handwriting so it can be read easily. When the moment arrives, the poem should be read slowly. It may also be easier to deliver the tribute without making eye contact with the audience.

Remember that the tribute should be simple and meaningful, so that the feelings and experiences of the person giving the tribute are conveyed. I hope this book helps you find a voice to express your grief and to honor your loved one.

In the event this book is revised for a second edition, I would welcome suggestions for other poems and readings. Please write to me in care of the publisher.

CHAPTER ONE:
EARTH IS YOUR MOTHER
Tributes to Mothers

I dream once more I sit upon your knee,
And hear sweet counsel that I should not grieve.
—Max Ehrmann

No person ever really recovers from the loss of a mother. Child or adult, no matter what age, becomes an orphan, certainly in his or her mind, and sometimes to others. Sons lose their first love; daughters lose a large piece of themselves as girls, as women, and as the mothers they are or will be. It is therefore one of the most difficult tasks of the bereaved to put a voice to the significance of this loss. *You move in all my gestures, all my silences.* To properly honor this person that has meant so much to one's own being is a daunting challenge. The readings that follow are some writers' attempts to give shape to the depth of that deprivation, yet still celebrate the soul of that one person who in so many ways lives on in others—*yours shall be the love that never dies.* As Julius Lester said in his essay on grief, "Death ends a life but death does not end a relationship."

Additional poems that may be appropriate can be found in Chapter Ten (women) and Chapter Eleven (general tributes).

Kaddish

Mother of my birth, for how long were we together
in your love and my adoration of your self?
For the shadow of a moment as I breathed your pain
and you breathed my suffering, as we knew
of shadows in lit rooms that would swallow the light.

Your face beneath the oxygen tent was alive
but your eyes were closed. Your breathing was hoarse
but your sleep was with death. I was alone with you
as it was when I was young but only alone now
and now with you. I was to be alone forever
as I was learning, watching you become alone.

Earth is your mother as you were mine, my earth,
my sustenance, my comfort and my strength
and now without you turn to your mother
and seek from her that I may meet you again
in rock and stone: whisper to the stone,
I love you; whisper to the rock, I found you;
whisper to earth, Mother, I have found my mother
and I am safe and always have been.

—David Ignatow (1914–1997)

In Memory of My Mother

I do not think of you lying in the wet clay
Of a Monaghan graveyard; I see
You walking down a lane among the poplars
On your way to the station, or happily

Going to second Mass on a summer Sunday—
You meet me and you say:
"Don't forget to see about the cattle—"
Among your earthiest words the angels stray.

And I think of you walking along a headland
Of green oats in June,
So full of repose, so rich with life—
And I see us meeting at the end of a town

On a fair day by accident, after
The bargains are all made and we can walk
Together through the shops and stalls and markets
Free in the oriental streets of thought.

O you are not lying in the wet clay,
For it is a harvest evening now and we
Are piling up the rocks against the moonlight
And you smile up at us—eternally.

—Patrick Kavanagh (1905–1969)

For a Dead Lady

No more with overflowing light
Shall fill the eyes that now are faded,
Nor shall another's fringe with night
Their woman-hidden world as they did.

No more shall quiver down the days
The flowing wonder of her ways,
Whereof no language may requite
The shifting and the many-shaded.

The grace, divine, definitive,
Clings only as a faint forestalling;
The laugh that love could not forgive
Is hushed, and answers to no calling;
The forehead and the little ears
Have gone where Saturn keeps the years;
The breast where roses could not live
Has done with rising and with falling.

The beauty, shattered by the laws
That have creation in their keeping,
No longer trembles at applause,
Or over children that are sleeping;
And we who delve in beauty's lore
Know all that we have known before
Of what inexorable cause
Makes Time so vicious in his reaping.

—Edwin Arlington Robinson (1869–1935)

Mother

Never a sigh for the cares that she bore for me,
Never a thought of the joys that flew by;
Her one regret that she couldn't do more for me,
Thoughtless and selfish, her Master was I.

Oh, the long nights that she came at my call to me!
Oh, the soft touch of her hands on my brow!
Oh, the long years that she gave up her all to me!
Oh, how I yearn for her gentleness now!

Slave to her baby! Yes, that was the way of her,
Counting her greatest of services small;
Words cannot tell what this old heart would say of her,
Mother—sweetest and fairest of all.

—Edgar Albert Guest (1881–1959)

Mother

Again your kindly, smiling face I see.
Do I but dream? And do my eyes deceive?
Again you whisper through the years to me,
I feel the pressure of your lips at eve.
I dream once more I sit upon your knee,
And hear sweet counsel that I should not grieve,
My hand in yours at twilight time as we
Talk low, and I your sweet caress receive.
At times I see your face with sorrow wrung,
Until, somewhat confused, I scarce believe
That I still dream. Your friends when you were young,
Your own great hopes, your cheer and laughter free
In some weird way are strangely haunting me.
O mother of my childhood's pleasant days!
Still whispering courage and dispelling fears
In daylight hours or quiet moonlight rays,
Are you a dream come from my younger years?
Or do you really walk along the ways,
And know my triumphs, or my inner tears,
That quickly cease when you close by me seem?
Let me sleep on, dear God, if I but dream.

—Max Ehrmann (1872–1945)

The Mother

There will be a singing in your heart,
There will be a rapture in your eyes;
You will be a woman set apart,
You will be so wonderful and wise.
You will sleep, and when from dreams you start,
As of one that wakes in Paradise,
There will be a singing in your heart,
There will be a rapture in your eyes.

There will be a moaning in your heart,
There will be an anguish in your eyes;
You will see your dearest ones depart,
You will hear their quivering good-byes.
Yours will be the heart-ache and the smart,
Tears that scald and lonely sacrifice;
There will be a moaning in your heart,
There will be an anguish in your eyes.

There will come a glory in your eyes,
There will come a peace within your heart;
Sitting 'neath the quiet evening skies,
Time will dry the tear and dull the smart.
You will know that you have played your part;
Yours shall be the love that never dies:
You, with Heaven's peace within your heart,
You, with God's own glory in your eyes.

—*Robert W. Service (1874–1958)*

Mother Died Today

She walks in dreams
like nothing...
is a ghost
is a lover
in a locket.

She was everyday
now
once-in-a-while
very close at heart.

Memories wring out
dry out
to a plot
where the only lap
is a stone

or a couch
where 2 eyes
stared
passed me
scared me

dreaming
live
gasping

nothing now
but white
men-flowers-cousins
and a smell
that chills my love.

                    —Jean Lozoraitis

Mother in Gladness, Mother in Sorrow

Mother in gladness, Mother in sorrow,
Mother today, and Mother tomorrow,
With arms ever open to fold and caress you
O Mother of Mine, may God keep you and bless you.

                    —W. Dayton Wedgefarth

My Mother, Life

She came as a falling star to the lakes. She the lithesome virgin not
to be turned into a tree, she who would never dress like a penguin.
An original want-not, she believed in philosophy, but she called it
faith. And so her talk entered my lungs and came out as a call to the
unnumerable vessels that are the wives of time.

Then there is the long span of silence. Every totem to acceptance she
wore as an accessory. While the tropic darkened palm wore its
microbe haunt she carried a burdened prose that was barely written,
never spoken. She could look and look, and never imagine the stimu-
lation of the lake when she saw the ocean themselves after every
rain, in sunlit rainbow. She had found a complex image that added
up. So she rested, and from her rest I derived my strength.

Consider open accidents of flesh, consider perfection of fur in a cat,
consider the curatorial mode of an almost wholly passed age, consider the feeling that has a character it emanates from. The fruit is no
more costly than its retrieval, the light it gets is subject to cultiva-
tion, the dark it needs is infallibly measured, and then there is cool.

—*John Godfrey (1945–)*

My Mother's Second Life

I hear about me your familiar step,
the pacings of clouds or a slow river;
your gentle pride and humble majesty
subjecting me to an eternal domination.

Over unforgotten reaches of pale time,
over green families prostrate on the earth,
over discarded costumes, the sad wardrobes
of a rainy country, you reign quietly.

You walk among insects and mushrooms,
your laws control my hands each day;
your voice runs furtively in mine
dissolving its ashes and base metals.

Compass of my journey in the world.
Origin of my blood, source of my destiny,
When earth had drawn your face to his,
I awoke surprised to find I was alive.

And I tried to break down invisible doors,
a prisoner who raged in vain.
On ropes of sobs I tried to hang myself;
Calling after you, I was swamped in dreams.

But you found new life inside me.
I feel you gently, gently breathing,
and so surmise a celestial order in
the sweet things guided by your hands.

You give full substance to the morning sun,
and with an old solicitude you wind me
in your bright, weightless cloak,
cool as cockerel morning and its shadows.

You count the liquid notes of insects and birds,
the sweetness of the world that comes to me;
your tender signals point the way I go;
in solitude I speak in your occult language.

You move in all my gestures, all my silences.
Over my shoulder you issue your commands.
When night soaks up all colors,
emptiness breathes your infinite presence.

I hear inside me your small prophecies,
and, by my side through all my vigils,
you still advise me on events, inscrutable codes,
the genesis of stars, the age of plants.

My heart in heaven, live, live without years.
My own first blood, my own first light,
may your immortal inspiration in all things
like a vast chorus surround me and sustain me.

—John Malcolm Brinnin (1916–)

CHAPTER TWO:
HE PLAYED THE GAME
Tributes to Fathers

So present in your absence.
—May Sarton

Whether your father was a close, loving presence in your life, or a remote, mostly absent parent, the effect this man had upon you is a lasting one. The patterns you established with him as you grew up shaped the person you became as an adult. The relationship he and your mother modeled for you became the die cast on your own associations with the opposite gender, whether by unintentional adoption or conscious rejection.

Paying tribute to your father at his funeral can be an opportunity to recognize his gifts to you—perhaps personality traits, technical ability, business acumen, or simply the time he spent with you. If it was not possible to do so during his lifetime, this may be the chance to apologize to him for long-ago misunderstandings or hasty words. Some find the memorial service the only moment in which the words "I love you" can be said to the man who may have found such outward displays of affection uncomfortable.

When looking for the poem that will acknowledge your father, don't restrict yourself to just the readings in this section of the book. If your father was a great friend to you, you may find what you need in the chapter on friends (Chapter Five). Your father's identity may have been strongly aligned as a soldier or veteran, in which case the memorials to soldiers in Chapter Seven could prove helpful. And of course, Chapter Nine (men) and Chapter Eleven (general tributes) should also be reviewed for appropriate material.

Do Not Go Gentle Into That Good Night

Do not go gentle into that good night,
Old age should burn and rave at close of day;
Rage, rage against the dying of the light.
Though wise men at their end know dark is right,
Because their words had forked no lightning they
Do not go gentle into that good night.

Good men, the last wave by, crying how bright
Their frail deeds might have danced in a green bay,
Rage, rage against the dying of the light.

Wild men who caught and sang the sun in flight,
And learn, too late, they grieved it on its way,
Do not go gentle into that good night.

Grave men, near death, who see with blinding sight
Blind eyes could blaze like meteors and be gay,
Rage, rage against the dying of the light.

And you, my father, there on the sad height,
Curse, bless, me now with your fierce tears, I pray.
Do not go gentle into that good night.
Rage, rage against the dying of the light.

> *—Dylan Thomas (1914–1953). Read by Kate Burton at the
> 1984 funeral of her father, the actor Richard Burton.*

Elegy
Charles Barber
1956–1992

So present in your absence
You will always be walking
Down the grassy path
Toward me,
Tall and smiling,
Not under the cruel spell
That has taken you away,
Blind and spent,

After the excruciating battle.
You will always be holding
My little dog tenderly
In your arms.
You will always be here with me
As long as I live,
A towering figure of love.

—May Sarton (1912–1995)

Nothing Is Lost

Nothing is lost.
We are too sad to know that, or too blind;
Only in visited moments do we understand:
It is not that the dead return—
They are about us always, though unguessed.

This penciled Latin verse
You dying wrote me, ten years past and more,
Brings you as much alive to me as the self you wrote it for,
Dear father, as I read your words
With no word but Alas.

Lines in a letter, lines in a face
Are faithful currents of life: the boy has written
His parents across his forehead, and as we burn
Our bodies up each seven years,
His own past self has left no plainer trace.

Nothing dies.
The cells pass on their secrets, we betray them
Unknowingly; in a freckle, in the way
We walk, recall some ancestor,
And Adam in the colour of our eyes.

Yes, on the face of the newborn,
Before the soul has taken full possession,
There pass, as over a screen, in succession
The images of other beings:
Face after face looks out, and then is gone.

Nothing is lost, for all in love survive.
I lay my cheek against his sleeping limbs
To feel if he is warm, and touch in him
Those children whom no shawl could warm,
No arms, no grief, no longing could revive.

Thus what we see, or know,
Is only a tiny portion, at the best,
Of the life in which we share; an iceberg's crest
Our sunlit present, our partial sense,
With deep supporting multitudes below.

      —Anne Ridler (1912–)

Requiem

Under the wide and starry sky,
Dig the grave and let me lie.
Glad did I live and gladly die,
And I laid me down with a will.

This be the verse you gave for me:
Here he lies where he longed to be;
Home is the sailor, home from the sea,
And the hunter home from the hill.

      —Robert Louis Stevenson (1850–1894)

To His Dead Body

When roaring gloom surged inward and you cried,
Groping for friendly hands, and clutched, and died,
Like racing smoke, swift from your lolling head
Phantoms of thoughts and memory thinned and fled.

Yet, though my dreams that throng the darkened stair
Can bring me no report of how you fare,
Safe quit of wars, I speed you on your way,
Slow-rising, saintless, confident and kind—
Dear, red-faced father God who lit your mind.

      —Siegfried Sassoon (1886–1967)

To His Son, Vincent Corbet

What I shall leave thee none can tell,
but all shall say I wish thee well.
I wish then, Vin, before all wealth,
Both bodily and ghostly health;
Not too much wealth, nor wit, come to thee,
So much of either may undo thee.
I wish thee learning not for show,
Enough for to instruct and know—
Not such as gentlemen require
To prate at table or at fire.

I wish thee all thy mother's graces,
Thy father's fortunes and his places.
I wish thee friends, and one at court,
Not to build on, but support,
To keep thee, not in doing many
Oppressions, but from suffering any.
I wish thee peace in all thy ways,
Nor lazy nor contentious days,
And when thy soul and body part,
As innocent as now thou art.

—Richard Corbet (1582–1635)

To W.P.:II

With you a part of me hath passed away;
For in the peopled forest of my mind
A tree made leafless by this wintry wind
Shall never don again its green array.
Chapel and fireside, country road and bay,
Have something of their friendliness resigned;
Another, if I would, I could not find,
And I am grown much older in a day.
But yet I treasure in my memory
Your gift of charity, and young heart's ease,
And the dear honor of your amity;
For these once mine, my life is rich with these.
And I scarce know which part may greater be,—
What I keep of you, or you rob from me.

—George Santayana (1863–1952)

CHAPTER THREE:
FAIRWELL, FAIR FLOWER
Tributes to Children

Songs of the Death of Children (Kindertotenlieder) by Friedrich Rückert
The Soul by Author Unknown
Stillborn by Dennis O'Driscoll
Surprised by Joy by William Wordsworth
To All Parents by Edgar Albert Guest
To Daffodils by Robert Herrick
The Unknown Child by Elizabeth Jennings
Warm Summer Sun by Robert Richardson
Why God Takes Children by Author Unknown

I've lived the parting hour to see
Of one I would have died to save.
—Charlotte Brontë

The unthinkable, unspeakable loss of one's child. What words could possibly be adequate to say what should never have to be said? *She had always expected to gain the end of the path of life before you.*

Included in this section are memorials that are appropriate for miscarriages, abortions, and stillborns. Grief for a life that could have been is hard, lonely, unrelenting grief. Listen to the soul-wrenching cries from the authors of these readings, and you may find a way to express your own unbearable pain. *Without you, no rose can grow.*

April Burial

On this chill day
Let earth be warm,
Receiving the child,
Undoing the harm.

Death was by day.
Then let no light
Enter this grave,
This natural night.

Beneath all days
Leave these together:
Earth and the quick girl,
Quiet forever.

—Mark Van Doren (1894–1973)

At David's Grave

Yes, he is here in this
open field, in sunlight, among
the few young trees set out
to modify the bare facts—

he's here, but only
because we are here.
When we go, he goes with us

to be your hands that never
do violence, your eyes
that wonder, your lives

that daily praise life
by living it, by laughter.

He is never alone here,
never cold in the field of graves.

—Denise Levertov (1923–1997)

Death of a Son

My son, listen once more to the words of your mother. You were brought into life with her pains. You were nourished with her life. She has attempted to be faithful in raising you up. When you were young she loved you as her life. Your presence has been a source of great joy to her. Upon you she depended for support and comfort in her declining days. She had always expected to gain the end of the path of life before you. But you have outstripped her, and gone before her. Our great and wise creator has ordered it thus. By his will I am left to taste more of the miseries of this world. Your friends and relatives have gathered about your body, to look upon you for the last time. They mourn, as with one mind, your departure from among us. We, too, have but a few days more, and our journey shall be ended. We part now, and you are conveyed from our sight. But we shall soon meet again, and shall again look upon each other. Then we shall part no more. Our maker has called you to his home. Thither will we follow. So be it.

—Translated from the Iroquois by Ely S. Parker (1851)

Delia

Sweet as the tender fragrance that survives,
When martyred flowers breathe out their little lives,
Sweet as a song that once consoled our pain,
But never will be sung to us again,
Is thy remembrance. Now the hour of rest
Hath come to thee. Sleep, darling; it is best.

—Henry Wadsworth Longfellow (1807–1882)

Disappeared Child

If only I could wrest you out of nothing,
Muscle and fat, with every hair intact,
And give you back this painful air we breathe.

Or else I ought not to have conceived,
Wrapped in those sinews I was taught to love,
Nailed by a martyred madman.

To let you go this way, naive and terrible
Into the scream of silence in my head!
You are not there...Nor were you ever there.

Every move to contemplate the passing of cell to cell—
Which girdled round, becomes in your flesh
The woman measured into the child—

Is blind seeing; calling to the blind,
To find that which was not; was inward;
The light of darkness which lies everywhere.

> —*Ruth Stone*

Epitaph on a Child

Here, freed from pain, secure from misery, lies
A child, the darling of his parents' eyes:
A gentler Lamb ne'er sported on the plain,
A fairer flower will never bloom again:
Few were the days allotted to his breath;
Now let him sleep in peace his night of death.

> —*Thomas Gray (1716–1771)*

Epitaph on Salathiel Pavy
A Child of Queen Elizabeth's Chapel

Weep with me, all you that read
        This little story;
And know, for whom a tear you shed
        Death's self is sorry.
'Twas a child that so did thrive
        In grace and feature,
As Heaven and Nature seemed to strive
        Which owned the creature.
Years he numbered scarce thirteen
        When Fates turned cruel,
Yet three filled Zodiacs had he been
        The Stage's jewel;
And did act (what now we moan)
        Old men so duly,

As sooth the Parcae thought him one,
    He played so truly.
So, by error, to his fate
    They all consented;
But, viewing him since, alas, too late!
    They have repented;
And have sought, to give new birth,
    In baths to steep him;
But, being so much too good for earth,
    Heaven vows to keep him.

    —Ben Jonson (1572–1637)

For a Child Born Dead

What ceremony can we fit
You into now? If you had come
Out of a warm and noisy room
To this, there'd be an opposite
For us to know you by. We could
Imagine you in a lively mood

And then look at the other side,
The mood drawn out of you, the breath
Defeated by the power of death.
But we have never seen you stride
Ambitiously the world we know.
You could not come and yet you go.

But there is nothing now to mar
Your clear refusal of our world.
Not in our memories can we mould
You or distort your character.
Then all our consolation is
That grief can be as pure as this.

    —Elizabeth Jennings (1926–)

For a First Christmas in Heaven

You see, dear Lord, she never had a Christmas,
(She was so small when she came Home to You...)
This was to be her very first on earth—
(And I had planned so many things to do...)
Behind the kitchen door still hides the tree.
I had been counting days till Christmas night—
We wanted so to watch her first surprise,
And see her little eyes grow big and bright...
For her first Christmas Eve, please, kindly Lord,
Plant on some tufty cloud a tiny tree...
Have some young angel trim it bright with stars,
And light one little candle...please, for me.

—Rosa Zagnoni Marinoni (1888?–1970)

In Memoriam

The long day sped;
A roof; a bed;
No years;
No tears.

—Lizette Woodworth Reese (1865–1935)

In Memoriam F.A.S.

Yet, O stricken heart, remember, O remember
How of human days he lived the better part.
April came to bloom and never dim December
Breathed its killing chills upon the head or heart.

Doomed to know not winter, only Spring, a being
Trod the flowery April blithely for awhile,
Took his fill of music, joy of thought and seeing,
Came and stayed and went, nor ever ceased to smile.

Came and stayed and went, and now when all is finished,
You alone have crossed the melancholy stream,
Yours the pang, but his, O his, the undiminished
Undecaying gladness, undeparted dream.

All that life contains of torture, toil, and treason,
Shame, dishonour, death, to him were but a name.
Here, a boy, he dwelt through all the singing season
And ere the day of sorrow departed as he came.

       —Robert Louis Stevenson (1850–1894)

In Memory of My Dear Grandchild Elizabeth Bradstreet, Who Deceased August, 1665 Being a Year and a Half Old

Farewell, dear babe, my heart's too much content,
Farewell, sweet babe, the pleasure of mine eye,
Farewell fair flower that for a space was lent,
Then ta'en away unto eternity.
Blest babe, why should I once bewail thy fate,
Or sigh thy days so soon terminate,
Till thou art settled in an everlasting state.

By nature trees do rot when they are grown,
And plums and apples thoroughly ripe do fall,
And corn and grass are in their season mown,
And time brings down what is both strong and tall.
But plants new set to be eradicate,
And buds new blown to have so short a date,
Is by his hand alone that guides nature and fate.

       —Anne Bradstreet (1612?–1672)

Little Elegy

Without you
No rose can grow;
No leaf be green
If never seen
Your sweetest face;
No bird have grace
Or power to sing;
Or anything
Be kind, or fair,
And you nowhere.

       —Elinor Hoyt Wylie (1885–1928)

Little Elegy for Gertrude Stein

Pass gently, pigeons on the grass,
For where she lies alone, alas,
Is all the wonder ever was.

Deeply she sleeps where everywhere
Grave children make pink marks on air
Or draw one black line...here to there.

Because effects were upside down,
Ends by knotty meanings thrown,
Words in her hands grew smooth as stone.

May every bell that says farewell,
Tolling her past all telling tell
What she, all told, knew very well.

If now, somehow, they try to say—
This way, that way, everywhichway—
Goodbye...the word is worlds away.

Come softly, all; she lies with those
Whose deepening innocence, God knows,
Is as the rose that is a rose.

—John Malcolm Brinnin (1916–)

The Mother

you were my child, my own,
until Death kidnapped you.
I have ransomed you at a fearful price:
goaded by implacable loss, I shall bring
new shoes to your graveside:
come out of your little wooden house
that has no windows
put on these bright shoes, my darling,
run with me
to a leafy secret place I have prepared
where all your griefs will be erased
your imperfections humored
and Life shall never find us out again.

—Hannah Alexander

Mother-Loss

If I could find one word
that would shudder the air
like that frightened sob,
that wordless prayer
of my newly-born,
who drew one breath,
and with unopened eyes
sank back into death;
If I could break the world's cold heart
with that cry,
then this grief would lift
and I could die.

—*Kenneth L. Patton*

On My First Son

Farewell, thou child of my right hand, and joy;
      My sin was too much hope of thee, loved boy.
Seven years thou wert lent to me, and I thee pay,
      Exacted by thy fate, on the just day.
Oh, could I lose all father now! for why
      Will man lament the state he should envy?
To have so soon 'scaped world's and flesh's rage,
      And, if no other misery, yet age?
Rest in soft peace, and asked, say, here doth lie
      Ben Jonson his best piece of poetry.
For whose sake henceforth all his vows be such,
      As what he loves may never like too much.

—*Ben Jonson (1572–1637)*

On the Death of Anne Bronte

There's little joy in life for me,
And little terror in the grave;
I've lived the parting hour to see
Of one I would have died to save.

Calmly to watch the failing breath,
Wishing each sigh might be the last;
Longing to see the shade of death
O'er those beloved features cast;

The cloud, the stillness that must part
The darling of my life from me;
And then to thank God from my heart,
To thank him well and fervently;

Although I knew that we had lost
The hope and glory of our life;
And now, benighted, tempest-tossed,
Must bear alone the weary strife.

> —*Charlotte Brontë (1816–1855)*

Remember

Remember me when I am gone away,
Gone far away into the silent land;
When you can no more hold me by the hand,
Nor I half turn to go, yet turning stay.
Remember me when no more, day by day,
You tell me of our future that you planned:
Only remember me; you understand
It will be late to counsel then or pray.
Yet if you should forget me for a while
And afterwards remember, do not grieve:
For if the darkness and corruption leave
A vestige of the thoughts that once I had,
Better by far you should forget and smile
Than that you should remember and be sad.

> —*Christina Georgina Rossetti (1830–1894)*

Songs of the Death of Children (Kindertotenlieder)

You must not shut the night inside you,
But endlessly in light the dark immerse.
A tiny lamp has gone out in my tent—
I bless the flame that warms the universe.

> —*Friedrich Rückert (1788–1866)*

The Soul

A lone and alone and lonely
The night wind calls to me.
Pulling me away from my reality
To a place that is quiet and free.

Have you no arms to comfort you?
The wind would whisper to me.
Have you no soul that understands
The waves that trouble your sea?

A child begins life unknowing
What twists of the road he will take.
And as he grows he comes closer
To the home he has left behind.

Come back, come back, call the angels.
Your time spent here is done.
Return to the souls who love you.
Return to the home of the sun.
One taste of bitter sweet elixir
And the soul begins to fly.
Set free from the bonds and the shackles.
Set free to soar through the sky.

Away, away to the brightest day
Away from the cares of this world.
Slip, slip, slipping away
Goes a soul too weary to stay.

Pity the tears of an unborn child
Who cries for the life he will lead.
Or even more so, for the tears of a soul
Who has lived and has need to leave.

—*Author Unknown*

Stillborn

what we are lamenting
is what has not been
and what will not have seen
this mild May morning

what we are lamenting
is unsuckled air
and what was brought to bear
this mild May morning

what we are lamenting
is the blood and puppy fat, our child,
that has not laughed or cried
this mild May mourning

what we are lamenting
is the life we crave
snatched from the cradle to the grave
this mild May morning.

—*Dennis O'Driscoll (1954–)*

Surprised by Joy

Surprised by joy—impatient as the wind
      I turned to share the transport—Oh! with whom
      But thee, deep buried in the silent tomb,
That spot which no vicissitude can find
Love, faithful love, recalled thee to my mind—
      But how could I forget thee? Through what power,
      Even for the least division of an hour,
Have I been so beguiled as to be blind
To my most grievous loss!—That thought's return
      Was the worst pang that sorrow ever bore,
Save one, one only, when I stood forlorn,
      Knowing my heart's best treasure was no more;
That neither present time, nor years unborn
      Could to my sight that heavenly face restore.

—*William Wordsworth (1770–1850)*

To All Parents

"I'll lend you for a little time a child of Mine," He said,
"For you to love the while she lives and mourn for when she's dead.
It may be six or seven years, or twenty-two or three.
But will you, till I call her back, take care of her for Me?
She'll bring her charms to gladden you, and shall her stay be brief
You'll have her lovely memories as solace for your grief.

I cannot promise she will stay, since all from earth return,
But there are lessons taught down there I want this child to learn.
I've looked the wide world over in my search for teachers true
And from the throngs that crowd life's lanes I have selected you.
Now will you give her all your love, nor think the labor vain,
Nor hate Me when I come to call to take her back again?"

I fancied that I heard them say, "Dear Lord, Thy will be done!
For all the joys Thy child shall bring, the risk of grief we'll run.
We'll shelter her with tenderness, we'll love her while we may,
And for the happiness we've known forever grateful stay;
But should the angels call for her much sooner than we've planned,
We'll brave the bitter grief that comes and try to understand."

— *Edgar Albert Guest (1881–1959)*

To Daffodils

Fair Daffodils, we weep to see
You haste away so soon;
As yet the early-rising sun
Has not attain'd his noon.
Stay, stay,
Until the hasting day
Has run
But to the even-song;
And, having pray'd together, we
Will go with you along.

We have short time to stay, as you,
We have as short a spring;
As quick a growth to meet decay,
As you, or anything.
We die
As your hours do, and dry
Away,
Like to the summer's rain;
Or as the pearls of morning's dew,
Ne'er to be found again.

— *Robert Herrick (1591–1674)*

The Unknown Child

The child will never lie in me, and you
Will never be its father. Mirrors must
Replace the real image, make it true
So that the gentle love-making we do
Has powerful passions and a parents' trust

The child will never lie in me and make
Our loving careful. We must kiss and touch
Quietly, watch our own reflexions break
As in a pool that is disturbed. Oh take
My watchful love; there must not be too much

A child lies within my mind. I see
the eyes, the hands. I see you also there.
I see you waiting with an honest care,
Within my mind, within me bodily,
And birth and death close to us constantly.

>   —*Elizabeth Jennings (1926–)*

Warm Summer Sun

Warm summer sun,
  Shine kindly here;
Warm southern wind,
  Blow softly here;
Green sod above,
  Lie light, lie light—
Good-night, dear heart,
  Good-night,
  good-night.

>   —*Robert Richardson (1855–1901). Read by Samuel Clemens*
>   *(Mark Twain) on the death of his daughter Susy.*

Why God Takes Children

When God calls little children to dwell with Him above
We mortals sometimes question the wisdom of His love
For no heartache compares with the death of one small child.
Who does so much to make our world seem so wonderful and mild.

Perhaps God tires of calling the aged to His fold.
So He picks a rosebud before it can grow old.
God knows how much we need them, and so He takes but few.
To make the land of heaven more beautiful to view.
Believing this is difficult still somehow we must try.
The saddest word mankind knows will always be Good-bye.
So when a little child departs we who are left behind,
Must realize God loves children.
Angels are hard to find!

   —Author Unknown

CHAPTER FOUR:
THIS IS MY HEARTH
Tributes to Soul Mates, Spouses and Lovers

I remember someone I love.
The first meaning of that sentence is that the loved one is gone.
—David J. Wolpe

Unlike a blood relative such as a father, sister or son, a soul mate is chosen. Staying together, in an age of numerous and fleeting relationships, is an act of courage, faith and love. When a relationship between two adults endures, the passing of one leaves a breach like no other. And if the words "till death do us part" are actually observed, the end of one spouse is the end of a way of life.

There are other sections of this book that may help you find the right words to say at your loved one's memorial service. The readings found in Chapter Five (friends) are relevant for anyone who considers their lover or spouse to also be their friend. Refer to Chapter Nine (men) or Chapter Ten (women) and to the general tributes (Chapter Eleven) for additional readings.

And Not My Wounds

Tell him I was beautiful,
Tell him I walked well;
Tell him I was columbine,
Brown daisy, and harebell.

He talked of these things that I was,
And called the world to see,
Like one who had created them,
Then manufactured me.

Tell him I am stars by night,
And stillness by noonday.
For he must know, that left me here,
Nothing has gone away;

Nothing is dead or different—
Tell him, and make sure.
For he must understand that I
And not my wounds endure.

—Mark Van Doren (1894–1973)

As Long As I Continue Weeping

As long as I continue weeping
Tears for our past happiness,
As long as, sounds of grief suppressed,
My voice comes clearly singing,
As long as tender hands in fingering
The gentle lute can ring your praise,
As long as peace my soul allays,
Contented truly with your understanding,
Then I do not wish to die.
But when I feel my eyes grow dry,
My voice grow hoarse, my hand grow slack,
And on this mortal earth my spirit lack
A sign of love's quick life,
Then, Death, please turn my day to night.

—Louise Labe (1526?–1566)

Bright Is the Ring of Words

Bright is the ring of words
When the right man rings them,
Fair the fall of songs
When the singer sings them.
Still they are carolled and said—
On wings they are carried—
After the singer is dead
And the maker buried.

Low as the singer lies
In the field of heather,
Songs of his fashion bring
The swains together.
And when the west is red
With the sunset embers,
The lover lingers and sings
And the maid remembers.

—Robert Louis Stevenson (1850–1894). Read by actor
Henry Fonda at the 1968 funeral of author John Steinbeck.

Code Poem for the French Resistance

The life that I have is all that I have,
And the life that I have is yours.
The love that I have of the life that I have
Is yours and yours and yours.

A sleep I shall have
A rest I shall have,
Yet death will be but a pause.
For the peace of my years in the long green grass
Will be yours and yours and yours.

—Leo Marks. Recited in the 1958 film Carve Her Name with
Pride, *based on the book by R. J. Minney.*

Death in Absentia
for Carole Slader

In the structure of her veins
I found the pulse of her fortune.
She's found the secret of the moths
Traced in wet earthworm trails.
Yes, the weakness of the living
Is in attaching importance
To the bones of the dead
But, oh, the line between life and death
Is not where we thought it was.
Dead, my love?
Like a pebble in my shoe
I'll walk with you for the remainder of my days.
Dead, my love.

—*Rita Mae Brown (1944–)*

Elegy on the Death of Her Husband

In sad and ashy weeds I sigh,
I groan, I pine, I mourn;
My oaten yellow reeds
I all to jet and ebon turn.
My wat'ry eyes, like winter's skies,
My furrowed cheeks o'erflow.
All heavens know why men mourn as I,
And who can blame my woe?

In sable robes of night my days
Of joy consumed be;
My sorrow sees no light;
My lights through sorrow nothing see:
For now my sun his course hath run,
And from his sphere doth go,
To endless bed of soldered lead,
And who can blame my woe?

My flocks I now forsake, that so
My sheep my grief may know;
The lilies loath to take

That since his death presum'd to grow.
I envy air because it dare
Still breathe, and he not so;
Hate earth, that doth entomb his youth,
And who can blame my woe?

Not I, poor I alone—(alone
How can this sorrow be?)
Not only men make moan, but
More than men make moan with me:
The gods of greens, the mountain queens,
The fairy circles row,
The muses nine, and powers divine,
Do all condole my woe.

—*Anne Howard, Duchess of Arundel (1557–1630)*

Farewell

Good-bye!—no, do not grieve that it is over,
The perfect hour;
That the winged joy, sweet honey-loving rover,
Flits from the flower.

Grieve not—it is the law. Love will be flying—
Yes, love and all.
Glad was the living—blessed by the dying.
Let the leaves all.

—*Harriet Monroe (1860–1936)*

For My Wife, Wanda: Love Will Never Go Away

Spring, and the land lies fresh-green
Beneath a yellow sun.
We walked the land together, you and I
And never knew what future days would bring.
Will you often think of me,
When flowers burst forth each year?
When the earth begins to grow again?
Some say death is so final.

But my love for you can never die.
Just as the sun once warmed our hearts,
Let this love touch you some night,
When I am gone,
And loneliness comes—
Before the dawn begins to scatter
Your dreams away.

Summer, and I never knew a bird
Could sing so sweet and clear,
Until they told me I must leave you
For a while.
I never knew the sky could be so deep a blue,
Until I knew I could not grow old with you.
But better to be loved by you,
Than to have lived a million summers,
And never known your love.
Together, let us, you and I
Remember the days and nights,
For eternity.

Fall, and the earth begins to die,
And leaves turn golden-brown upon the trees.
Remember me, too, in autumn, for I will walk with you,
As of old, along a city sidewalk at evening-time,
Though I cannot hold you by the hand.

Winter, and perhaps someday there may be
Another fireplace, another room,
With crackling fire and fragrant smoke,
And turning, suddenly we will be together,
And I will hear your laughter and touch your face,
And hold you close to me again.
But, until then, if loneliness should seek you out,
Some winter night, when snow is falling down,
Remember, though death has come to me,
Love will never go away!

    —Orville E. Kelly (1931–)

For This Is Wisdom

For this is Wisdom; to love, to live,
To take what Fate, or the Gods, may give,
To ask no question, to make no prayer,
To kiss the lips and caress the hair,
Speed passion's ebb as you greet its flow,—
to have, —to hold, —and, —in time, —let go!

—*Laurence Hope (1865–1904)*

From *Discordants*

Music I heard with you was more than music,
And bread I broke with you was more than bread.
Now that I am without you, all is desolate,
All that was once so beautiful is dead.

Your hands once touched this table and this silver,
And I have seen your fingers hold this glass.
These things do not remember you, beloved:
And yet your touch upon them will not pass.

For it was in my heart you moved them,
And blessed them with your hands and with your eyes.
And in my heart they will remember always:
They knew you once, O beautiful and wise!

—*Conrad Aiken (1889–1973)*

Funeral Blues

Stop all the clocks, cut off the telephone,
Prevent the dog from barking with a juicy bone,
Silence the pianos and with muffled drum
Bring out the coffin, let the mourners come.

Let aeroplanes circle moaning overhead
Scribbling on the sky the message He Is Dead,
Put crepe bows round the white necks of the public doves,
Let the traffic policemen wear black cotton gloves.

He was my North, my South, my East and West,
My working week and my Sunday rest,
My noon, my midnight, my talk, my song;
I thought that love would last for ever: I was wrong.

The stars are not wanted now; put out every one:
Pack up the moon and dismantle the sun;
Pour away the ocean and sweep up the woods:
For nothing now can ever come to any good.

> —*Wystan Hugh Auden (1907–1973). Read in the 1994 film*
> Four Weddings and a Funeral.

Last Words

I knew not twas so dire a crime
To say the word, "Adieu";
But this shall be the only time
My lips or heart shall sue.

The wild hillside, the winter morn,
The gnarled and ancient tree,
If in your breast they waken scorn,
Shall wake the same in me.
I can forget black eyes and brows,
And lips of falsest charm,
If you forget the sacred vows
Those faithless lips could form.

If hard commands can tame your love,
Or strongest walls can hold,
I would not wish to grieve above
A thing so false and cold.

And there are bosoms bound to mine
With links both tried and strong;
And there are eyes whose lightning shine
Has warmed and blest me long:

Those eyes shall make my only day,
Shall set my spirit free,
And chase the foolish thoughts away
That mourn your memory.

> —*Emily Jane Brontë (1818–1848)*

Memory

I have a room whereinto no one enters
  Save I myself alone:
  There sits a blessed memory on a throne,
There my life centres.

While winter comes and goes—oh tedious comer!—
  And while its nip-wind blows;
  While bloom the bloodless lily and warm rose
Of lavish summer.

If any should force entrance he might see there
  One buried yet not dead,
  Before whose face I no more bow my head
Or bend my knee there;

But often in my worn life's autumn weather
  I watch there with clear eyes,
  And think how it will be in Paradise
When we're together.

   —*Christina Georgina Rossetti (1830–1894)*

Now Voyager

Now voyager, lay here your dazzled head.
Come back to earth from air, be nourished.
Not with that light on light, but with this bread.

Here close to earth be cherished, mortal heart,
Hold your way deep as roots push rocks apart
To bring the spurt of green up from the dark.

Where music thundered let the mind be still,
Where the will triumphed let there be no will,
What light revealed, now let the dark fulfill.

Here close to earth the deeper pulse is stirred,
Here where no wings rush and no sudden bird,
But only heart-beat upon beat is heard.

Here let the fiery burden be all spilled,
The passionate voice at last be calmed and stilled
And the long yearning of the blood fulfilled.

Now voyager, come home, come home to rest,
Here on the long-lost country of earth's breast
Lay down the fiery vision, and be blest, be blest.

> —*May Sarton (1912–1995)*

Ode: Intimations of Immortality from Recollections of Early Childhood

X

Then sing, ye Birds, sing a joyous song!
>   And let the young Lambs bound
>   As to the tabor's sound!
We in thought will join your throng,
>   Ye that pipe and ye that play,
>   Ye that through your hearts today
>   Fell the gladness of the May!
What though the radiance which was once so bright
Be now for ever taken from my sight,
>   Though nothing can bring back the hour
Of splendor in the grass, of glory in the flower;
>   We will grieve not, rather find
>   Strength in what is left behind;
>   In the primal sympathy
>   Which having been must ever be;
>   In the soothing thoughts that spring
>   Out of human suffering;
>   In the faith that looks through death,
>   In years that bring the philosophic mind.

> —*William Wordsworth (1770–1850). Read by Natalie Wood
> in the 1961 film* Splendor in the Grass.

Remembrance

Cold in the earth—and the deep snow piled above thee,
Far, far removed, cold in the dreary grave!
Have I forgot, my only Love, to love thee,
Severed at last by Time's all-severing wave?

Now, when alone, do my thoughts no longer hover
Over the mountains, on that northern shore,
Resting their wings where heath and fern-leaves cover
That noble heart for ever, ever more?

Cold in the earth—and fifteen wild Decembers
From those brown hills, have melted into spring—
Faithful indeed is the spirit that remembers
After such years of change and suffering!

Sweet Love of youth, forgive if I forget thee,
While the world's tide is bearing me along:
Other desires and darker hopes beset me,
Hopes which obscure, but cannot do thee wrong!

No later light has lightened up my heaven;
No second morn has ever shone for me:
All my life's bliss from thy dear life was given—
All my life's bliss is in the grave with thee.

But, when the days of golden dreams had perished,
And even Despair was powerless to destroy,
Then did I learn how existence could be cherished,
Strengthened, and fed without the aid of joy;

Then did I check the tears of useless passion,
Weaned my young soul from yearning after thine;
Sternly denied its burning wish to hasten
Down to that tomb already more than mine!

And, even yet, I dare not let it languish,
Dare not indulge in memory's rapturous pain;
Once drinking deep of that divinest anguish,
How could I seek the empty world again?

  —Emily Brontë (1818–1848)

Remembrance

Under the apple bough
Love, in a dream of leaves,
Dreamed we of love, as now—
All that gives beauty or grieves.
Over the sad world then
Curved like the sky that bough;
I was in heaven then—
You are in heaven now.

—George Parsons Lathrop (1851–1898)

Should You Go First

Should you go first and I remain
    To walk the road alone
I'll live in memory's garden dear
    With happy days we've known
In Spring I'll wait for roses red,
    When fades the lilac blue,
In early Fall, when brown leaves call
    I'll catch a glimpse of you.

Should you go first and I remain
    For battles to be fought,
Each thing you've touched along the way
    Will be a hallowed spot.
I'll hear your voice, I'll see your smile,
    Though blindly I may grope,
The memory of your helping hand
    Will buoy me on with hope.

Should you go first and I remain
    To finish with the scroll,
No lengthn'ning shadows shall creep in
    To make this life seem droll.
We've known so much happiness,
    We've had our cup of joy,
And memory is one gift of God
    That death cannot destroy.

Should you go first and I remain,
   One thing I'd have you do:
Walk slowly down that long, lone path,
   For soon I'll follow you.
I'll want to know each step you take
   That I may take the same,
For some day down that lonely road
   You'll hear me call your name.

   —Albert Kennedy Rowswell

Song

When I am dead, my dearest,
Sing no sad songs for me;
Plant thou no roses at my head,
Nor shady cypress tree:
Be the green grass above me
With showers and dewdrops wet:
And if thou wilt, remember,
And if thou wilt, forget.

I shall not see the shadows,
I shall not feel the rain;
I shall not hear the nightingale
Sing on as if in pain:

And dreaming through the twilight
That doth not rise nor set,
Haply I may remember,
And haply may forget.

   *—Christina Georgina Rossetti (1830–1894). Recited in the
   1987 made-for-TV movie* When the Time Comes.

Song for the Last Act

Now that I have your face by heart, I look
Less at its features than its darkening frame
Where quince and melon, yellow as young flame,
Lie with quilled dahlias and the shepherd's crook.

Beyond, a garden. There, in insolent ease
The lead and marble figures watch the show
Of yet another summer loath to go
Although the scythes hang in the apple trees.

Now that I have your voice by heart, I look.

Now that I have your voice by heart, I read
In the black chords upon a dulling page
Music that is not meant for music's cage,
Whose emblems mix with words that shake and bleed.
The staves are shuttled over with a stark
Unprinted silence. In a double dream
I must spell out the storm, the running stream.
The beat's too swift. The notes shift in the dark.

Now that I have your voice by heart, I read.

Now that I have your heart by heart, I see
The wharves with their great ships and architraves;
The rigging and the cargo and the slaves
On a strange beach under a broken sky.
O not departure, but a voyage done!
The bales stand on the stone; the anchor weeps
Its red rust downward, and the long vine creeps
Beside the salt herb, in the lengthening sun.

Now that I have your heart by heart, I see.

> —*Louise Bogan (1897–1970)*

Sonnet LXXI

No longer mourn for me when I am dead
Than you shall hear the surly sullen bell
Give warning to the world that I am fled
From this vile world, with vilest worms to dwell:
Nay, if you read this line, remember not
The hand that writ it; for I love you so,
That I in your sweet thoughts would be forgot,
If thinking on me then should make you woe.
O, if, I say, you look upon this verse

When I perhaps compounded am with clay,
Do not so much as my poor name rehearse,
But let your love even with my life decay;
  Lest the wise world should look into your moan,
  And mock you with me after I am gone.

  —*William Shakespeare (1564–1616)*

Sunset on the Spire

All that I dream
 By day or night
Lives in that stream
 Of lovely light.
Here is the earth,
 And there is the spire;
This is my hearth,
 And that is my fire.
From the sun's dome
 I am shouted proof
That this is my home,
 And that is my roof.
Here is my food,
 And here is my drink,
And I am wooed
 From the moon's brink.
And the days go over,
 And the nights end;
Here is my lover,
 Here is my friend.
All that I
 Could ever ask
Wears that sky
 Like a thin gold mask.

  —*Elinor Wylie (1885–1928)*

To an Athlete Dying Young

The time you won your town the race
We chaired you through the market-place:
Man and boy stood cheering by
And home we brought you shoulder-high.

To-day, the road all runners come,
Shoulder-high we bring you home,
And set you at your threshold down.
Townsman of a stiller town.

Smart lad, to slip betimes away
From fields where glory does not stay
And early though the laurel grows
It withers quicker than the rose.

Eyes the shady night has shut
Cannot see the record cut
And silence sounds no worse than cheers
After earth has stopped the ears:

Now you will not swell the rout
Of lads that wore their honors out,
Runners whom renown outran
And the name died before the man.

So set, before its echoes fade,
The fleet foot on the sill of shade,
And hold to the low lintel up
The still-defended challenge-cup.

And round that early-laurelled head
Will flock to gaze the strengthless dead,
And find unwithered on its curls
The garland briefer than a girl's.

> —*A.E. Housman (1859–1936). Read by Meryl Streep in the
> 1985 film* Out of Africa.

To My Dear and Loving Husband

If ever two were one, then surely we.
If ever man were loved by wife, then thee;
If ever wife was happy in a man,
Compare with me, ye women, if you can.
I prize thy love more than whole mines of gold,
Or all the riches that the East doth hold.
My love is such that rivers cannot quench,
Nor aught but love from thee give recompense.
Thy love is such I can no way repay;
The heavens reward thee manifold, I pray.
Then while we live, in love let's so persever,
That when we live no more we may live ever.

—Anne Bradstreet (1612–1672)

We Never Said Farewell

We never said farewell, not even looked
       Our last upon each other, for no sign
Was made when we the linked chain unhooked
       And broke the level line.

And here we dwell together, side by side,
       Our places fixed for life upon the chart.
Two islands that the roaring seas divide
       Are not more far apart.

—Mary Elizabeth Coleridge (1861–1907)

Wherever I May Be

Wherever I may be
In the woods or in the fields
Whatever the hour of day
Be it dawn or the eventide
My heart still feels it yet
The eternal regret...
As I sink into my sleep

The absent one is near
Alone upon my couch
I feel his beloved touch
In work or in repose
We are forever close...

      —Mary, Queen of Scots (1542–1587)

CHAPTER FIVE:
OUR HEART'S FRIEND
Tributes to Friends

But if the while I think on thee, dear friend,
All losses are restor'd, and sorrows end.
—William Shakespeare

How many times have you heard, or yourself said, "She's closer to me than my own sister," or, "He's just like family?" Friends are the first people with whom we have a relationship after our parents and siblings, and those early beginnings often bring years of intimacy and shared joy. The person you call to tell about adolescent injustices or the letter of acceptance from college, the buddy you spend every Super Bowl Sunday with even if he lives halfway across the country, the only person who really understands your inner longings, wild moments and quiet agonies. Friends make life a reasonable place. To some of us, the closeness we feel with a special friend is unmatched by any other relationship, and may endure longer.

It is usually when a friend dies that one is compelled, for the first time, to give a eulogy or say a few words at the service. Within this small collection of readings are poems that allude to long or dear friendships, regardless of age or gender. For additional tributes for female or male friends, refer to Chapter Nine (men) and Chapter Ten (women). Don't overlook the general tributes in Chapter Eleven for lovely pieces such as *The Appeal.*

Auden's Funeral

to Christopher Isherwood

One among friends who stood above your grave
I cast a clod of earth from those heaped there
Down on the great brass-handled coffin lid.
It rattled on the oak like a door knocker.
And at that sound I saw your face beneath
Wedged in an oblong shadow under ground:
Flesh creased, eyes shut, jaw jutting,
And on the mouth a smile: triumph of one
Who has escaped from life-long colleagues roaring
For him to join their throng. He's still half with us
Conniving slyly, yet he knows he's gone
Into that cellar where they'll never find him,
Happy to be alone, his last work done,
Word freed from world, into a different wood.

—*Stephen Spender (1909–1995)*

Ballade of Dead Friends

As we the withered ferns
By the roadside lying,
Time, the jester, spurns
All our prayers and prying—
All our tears and sighing,
Sorrow, change, and woe—
All our where-and-whying
For friends that come and go.

Life awakes and burns,
Age and death defying,
Till at last it learns
All but Love is dying;
Love's the trade we're plying,
God has willed it so;
Shrouds are what we're buying
For friends that come and go.

Man forever yearns
For the thing that's flying.
Everywhere he turns,
Men to dust are drying—
Dust that wanders, eyeing
(With eyes that hardly glow)
New faces, dimly spying
For friends that come and go.

And thus we all are nighing
The truth we fear to know:
Death will end our crying
For friends that come and go.

—Edwin Arlington Robinson (1869–1935)

Because He Lived

Because he lived, next door a child
To see him coming often smiled,
And thought him her devoted friend
Who gladly gave her coins to spend.

Because he lived, a neighbor knew
A clump of tall delphiniums blue
And oriental poppies red
He'd given for a flower bed.

Because he lived, a man in need
Was grateful for a kindly deed
And ever after tried to be
As thoughtful and as fine as he.

Because he lived, ne'er great or proud
Or known to all the motley crowd,
A few there were whose tents were pitched
Near his who found their lives enriched.

—Edgar Albert Guest (1881–1959)

Elegy

Wander, my troubled soul, sigh 'mid the night thy pain,
While from my cloud-hung brow stream showers of briny rain;
My spirit flies the earth, the darkest gloom pervades,
Hovers around the dead, and mingles with the shades.

O! friend of my breast! thou'rt entomb'd within my heart,
I still to thee alone my inmost thoughts impart;
Solac'd no more by thee, vain is the power of song,
Sighs check each tuneful lay, and murmuring glide along.

Thou wert unto my soul what the sun is to my sight,
But thou art set in death, and I am lost in night;
All nature seems a void of element'ry strife,
Where the soul is all cloud, and fraught with pain all life.

When near thy faithful breast I heeded not the storm,
Nor thought of wasting time, nor death's consuming worm;
Thy genius woke my thought, as oft we stray'd alone,
And rais'd me to that heaven to which thou now art flown.

Silent oft I mourn, sad wandering 'mid the gloom,
Or on the sea-beat shore I weep my bitter doom;
To thee, among the bless'd, my feeble soul would soar,
And 'mid the starry spheres th' Almighty Pow'r adore.

—Ann Batten Cristall (1795)

Epitaph on a Friend

An honest man here lies at rest,
The friend of man, the friend of truth,
The friend of age, and guide of youth:
Few hearts like his, with virtue warm'd,
Few heads with knowledge so inform'd;
If there's another world, he lives in bliss;
If there is none, he made the best of this.

—Robert Burns (1759–1796)

Even Such Is Time

Even such is time that takes in trust
Our youth, our joys, our all we have,
And pays us but with age and dust,
Who in the dark and silent grave,
When we have wandered all our ways,
Shuts up the story of our days.
But from this earth, this grave, this dust,
My God shall raise me up, I trust.

—Sir Walter Alexander Raleigh (1861–1922)

Gone

About the little chambers of my heart
Friends have been coming—going—many a year.
   The doors stand open there.
Some, lightly stepping, enter; some depart.

Freely they come and freely go, at will.
The walls give back their laughter; all day long
   They fill the house with song.
One door alone is shut, one chamber still.

—Mary Coleridge (1861–1907)

Joyce: By Herself and Her Friends

If I should go before the rest of you
Break not a flower nor inscribe a stone,
Nor when I'm gone speak in a Sunday voice
But be the usual selves that I have known.
         Weep if you must,
         Parting is hell,
But life goes on,
So sing as well.

—Joyce Grenfell (1910–1979)

The Last Signal

Silently I footed by an uphill road
That led from my abode to a spot yew-boughed;
Yellowly the sun sloped low down to westward,
And dark was the east with cloud.

Then, amid the shadow of that livid sad east,
Where the light was least, and a gate stood wide,
Something flashed the fire of the sun that was facing it,
Like a brief blaze on that side.

Looking hard and harder I knew what it meant—
The sudden shine sent from the livid east scene;
It meant the west mirrored by the coffin of my friend there,
Turning to the road from his green,
To take his last journey forth—he who in his prime
Trudged so many a time from that gate athwart the land!
Thus a farewell to me he signalled on his grave-way,
As with a wave of his hand.

—*Thomas Hardy (1840–1928)*

LIV

With rue my heart is laden
  For golden friends I had,
For many a rose-lipt maiden
  And many a lightfoot lad.

By brooks too broad for leaping
  The lightfoot boys are laid;
The rose-lipt girls are sleeping
  In fields where roses fade.

—*A.E. (Alfred Edward) Housman (1859–1936)*

May 23, 1853

How different the ramrod jingle of the chewink or any bird's note sounds now at 5 PM in the cooler, stiller air, when also the humming of insects is more distinctly heard, and perchance some impurity has begun to sink to earth strained by the air! Or is it, perchance, to be referred to the cooler, more clarified and pensive state of the mind, when dews have begun to descend in it and clarify it? Chaste eve! A certain lateness in the sound, pleasing to hear, which releases me from the obligation to return in any particular season. I have passed the Rubicon of staying out. I have said to myself, that way is not homeward: I will wander further from what I have called my home – to the home which is forever inviting me. In such an hour the freedom of the woods is offered me, and the birds sing my dispensation. In dreams the links of life are united: we forget that our friends are dead; we know them as of old.

—Henry David Thoreau (1817–1862)

My Buried Friends

My buried friends can I forget or must the grave eternal sever?
I know them now as I did then and in my heart they live forever.
They loved me once with love sincere and never did their love
        deceive me,
But often in my conflicts here they'd rally quick round to relieve me.

*—Recorded by Sidney Robertson Cowell from the singing of
Charles Spencer, Crandon, Wisconsin, 1937.*

My Friends Are Little Lamps to Me

My friends are little lamps to me,
        Their radiance warms and cheers my ways.
And all my pathways dark and lone
        Is brightened by their rays.

I try to keep them bright by faith,
        And never let them dim with doubt,
For every time I lose a friend
        A little lamp goes out.

—Elizabeth Whittemore

Poem

This day when I lay my hope aside
Dawns with a single stone of light
That builds to a low meridian
Till noon, a bare pillar, is my own height,
As such I can measure it.

This place seems right to say goodbye,
Having only a centre, no east or west,
Where nothing is large and all is calm.
Its firmament is my own eye,
It fits the landscape of my palm.

Since time has majesty to be so meek,
And space comes tamely to the hand,
This person must do no less for sorrow,
This mourner must not be too grand
Nor strike on golden tablets beyond belief.
Let the pen lie where it has fainted,
The few black words it wrote
Were not set down to flatter grief.

—Hildegarde Flanner (1899–1987)

A Prayer

Give me work to do;
Give me health;
Give me joy in simple things.
Give me an eye for beauty,
A tongue for truth,
A heart that loves,
A mind that reasons,
A sympathy that understands;
Give me neither malice nor envy,
But a true kindness
And a noble common sense.
At the close of each day
Give me a book,
And a friend with whom
I can be silent.

—Author Unknown

The Rhyme of the Restless Ones

We couldn't sit and study for the law;
  The stagnation of a bank we couldn't stand;
For our riot blood was surging, and we didn't need much urging
  To excitements and excesses that are banned.
So we took to wine and drink and other things,
  And the devil in us struggled to be free;
Till our friends rose up in wrath, and they pointed out the path,
  And they paid our debts and packed us o'er the sea.

Oh, they shook us off and shipped us o'er the foam,
To the larger lands that lure a man to roam;
  And we took the chance they gave
  Of a far and foreign grave,
And we bade good-by for evermore to home.
And some of us are climbing on the peak,
  And some of us are camping on the plain;
By pine and palm you'll find us, with never claim to bind us,
  By track and trail you'll meet us once again.

We are fated serfs to freedom—sky and sea;
  We have failed where slummy cities overflow;
But the stranger ways of earth know our pride and know our worth,
  And we go into the dark as fighters go.

Yes, we go into the night as brave men go,
Though our faces they be often streaked with woe;
  Yet we're hard as cats to kill,
  And our hearts are reckless still,
And we've danced with death a dozen times or so.

And you'll find us in Alaska after gold,
  And you'll find us herding cattle in the South.
We like strong drink and fun, and, when the race is run,
  We often die with curses in our mouth.
We are wild as colts unbroke, but never mean.
  Of our sins we've shoulders broad to bear the blame;
But we'll never stay in town and we'll never settle down,
  And we'll never have an object or an aim.

No, there's that in us that time can never tame;
And life will always seem a careless game;
    And they'd better far forget—
    Those who say they love us yet—
Forget, blot out with bitterness our name.

    —Robert W. Service (1874–1958)

Sonnet XXX

When to the sessions of sweet silent thought
I summon up remembrance of things past,
I sigh the lack of many a thing I sought,
And with old woes new wail my dear time's waste.
Then can I drown an eye, unus'd to flow,
For precious friends hid in death's dateless night,
And weep afresh love's long since cancell'd woe,
And moan th' expense of many a vanish'd sight.
Then can I grieve at grievances foregone,
And heavily from woe to woe tell o'er
The sad account of fore-bemoaned moan,
Which I new pay as if not paid before.
    But if the while I think on thee, dear friend,
    All losses are restor'd, and sorrows end.

    —William Shakespeare (1564–1616)

Time in the World
for Jon Bergen

I was fourteen going on thirty when I met you.
I am just a guileless kid when I dream of you
And so are you.
I talk, you listen.
We walk down a hospital hallway; you hold my hand.
I worry that you are bleeding and might die of it.
We know you must go through one of those doors,
where I cannot follow.
You tell me have faith,
words up against my heart like a hand.

You offer the childlike part of our friendship again
and it reminds me of who I was.
Life seems less threatening.
I awaken, floating for some time in that world,
like a loose tooth in a child's smile.

   —Yaedi Ignatow (1956–)

CHAPTER SIX:
THOSE WHO WALK WITH ME
Tributes to Sisters and Brothers

Thy memory lasts both here and there,
And thou shalt live as long as we.
—Matthew Arnold

The relationship between two siblings, regardless of gender, birth order or age difference, is a special one. The common bonds are shared parents and shared history. The loss of a brother or sister means that childhood memories can no longer be analyzed or validated with the same hindsight. Details of daily life as children—the arguments, jokes, favorite shows, family holidays—will never be recalled in the same way again.

Becoming adults can sometimes mean estrangement—in thought or in distance—but this does not change the connection two sisters have with one another, or the attachment two brothers experienced, or the understanding of a brother and sister for their mutual past. Sometimes, the adult sibling is the only one left who can recall the deceased as a child, and it is entirely appropriate to recount anecdotes from the past as part of the eulogy.

In seeking the right words to express this pain and this loss, look also at Chapters Five (friends) and Eleven (general tributes), and at Chapter Ten (women) for a sister or Chapter Nine (men) for a brother. Poems such as *Turn Again to Life* and *When I Die* say much about love and memory that could be a reflection of the regard two siblings had for each other.

Catullus' Ode to His Brother

By ways remote and distant waters sped,
Brother, to thy sad grave-side am I come,
That I may give the last gifts to the dead
And vainly parley with thine ashes dumb;
Since she who now bestows and now denies
Hath taken thee, hapless brother, from mine eyes.

But lo! These gifts, the heirlooms of past years,
Are made sad things to grace thy coffin-shell,
Take them, all drenched with a brother's tears,
And, brother, for all time, hail and farewell.

            —*Gaius Valerius Catullus (87–c.54 BC)*

The First Grief

Oh! Call my brother back to me,
          I cannot play alone;
The summer comes with flower and bee—
          Where is my brother gone?

The butterfly is glancing bright
          Across the sunbeam's track;
I care not now to chase its flight—
          Oh! Call my brother back.

The flowers run wild—the flowers we sowed
          Around our garden tree;
Our vine is drooping with its load—
          Oh! Call him back to me.

He would not hear my voice, fair child!
          He may not come to thee;
The face that once like spring-time smiled
          On earth no more thou'lt see.

A rose's brief, bright life of joy,
          Such unto him was given'
Go—thou must play alone, my boy—
          Thy brother is in heaven!

And has he left the birds and flowers
  And must I call in vain;
And through the long, long summer hours,
  Will he not come again?

And by the brook, and in the glade,
  Are all our wandering o'er?
Oh! While my brother with me played,
  Would I had loved him more!

   —Felicia Dorothea Hemans (1793–1835)

From Goblin Market

For there is no friend like a sister
In calm or stormy weather;
To cheer one on the tedious way,
To fetch one if she goes astray,
To lift one if one totters down,
To strengthen whilst one stands.

   —Christina Georgina Rossetti (1830–1894)

Grief

Grief reached across the world to get me,
sadness carries me across seas and countries
to your grave, my brother,

to offer the only gift I still can give you—
words you will not hear.

Fortune has taken you from me. You.
No reason, nothing fair.
I didn't deserve losing you.

Now, in the silence since,
as is the ancient custom of our people,
I say the mourner's prayer,
do the final kindness.

Accept and understand it, brother.
My head aches from crying.
Forever, goodbye.

—*Gaius Valerius Catullus (87–c.54 BC)*

I Only Wanted You

They say memories are golden
Well maybe that is true.
I never wanted memories,
I only wanted you.

A million times I needed you,
A million times I cried.
If love alone could have saved you
You never would have died.

In life I loved you dearly,
In death I love you still.
In my heart you hold a place
No one could ever fill.

If tears could build a stairway
And heartache make a lane,
I'd walk the path to heaven
And bring you back again.

Our family chain is broken,
And nothing seems the same.
But as God calls us one by one,
The chain will link again.

—*Author Unknown*

Logs on the Hearth
A Memory of a Sister

The fire advances along the log
Of the tree we felled,
Which bloomed and bore striped apples by the peck
Till its last hour of bearing knelled.

The fork that first my hand would reach
And then my foot
In climbing upward inch by inch, lies now
Sawn, sapless, darkening with soot.

Where the bark chars is where, one year,
It was pruned, and bled—
Then overgrew the wound. But now, at last,
Its growings all have stagnated.

My fellow-climber rises dim
From her chilly grave—
Just as she was, her foot near mine on the bending limb,
Laughing, her young brown hand awave.

            —*Thomas Hardy (1840–1928)*

Sister's Gone

We shared a bond of time and place,
Our lives entwined like threads of lace.
Her mother, my mother, her father, mine.
We shared a room, a space in time.
Same time and place in the Universe,
All things were shared with sister first.
Who will I share with from now on?
Sister's gone, Sister's gone.

            —*Fleta Aday*

CHAPTER SEVEN: HOME IS THE SAILOR
Tributes to Soldiers

Upon his shield returning,
Borne from the field of honor
Where he fell.
—George Lunt

Membership in the armed forces can be the defining episode in a person's life. For some, other roles may be adopted—that of father, aunt or grandparent—but the time spent in the service is that person's identity forevermore. It would be a great honor to remember that person publicly with a tribute that refers to the military or to the sacrifices made on behalf of the country.

Though there are relatively few tributes to soldiers in this collection, the ones presented here read beautifully. Classic poems by Robert Service and Sir Walter Raleigh are never dated. In the general tributes found in Chapter Eleven, *I Think Continually* is also appropriate.

Closure: A Much Needed War
III

I believe somewhere, everywhere
there is the generic veteran
for whom no national border,
nor ethnic pride
is grand enough
to color his humanity.
I believe also,
that it is this world's
most brave champions
who dream of peace
and each country's truest sons
who must live for it.
And, therefore,
not this Veterans Day
nor the next
nor the one after that
will men and women of my heart
find closure for the war we fought
in a ceremony honoring the dead.
(We cherish them best who gave it all
by dedicating our lives to the living.)
For closure, if such exists,
comes only to the warrior.
The veteran, is of other matter.
Truth under fire
has tempered each veteran
of Every war
from one part warrior
and one part human being.
And for each of Us
(long before closure)
there remains one, much needed war.
One, last commitment
worthy of a lifetime—
to fight for peace
in each of our hearts
against the fierce enemies

of our darkest natures.
And to march in lock-step
with veterans of all wars
from all nations
for human dignity.

Then shall we pass in review
and each will hear
mankind whisper to the gods,
"There then, goes one of ours."

    —Steve Mason

Epitaph on General Gordon

Warrior of God, man's friend,
   and tyrant's foe,
Now somewhere dead far in the
   waste Soudan,
Though livest in all hearts, for all
   men know
this earth has never borne a
   nobler man.

    —Alfred, Lord Tennyson (1809–1892)

High Flight

Oh! I have slipped the surly bonds of earth
And danced the skies on laughter-silvered wings;
Sunward I've climbed and joined the tumbling mirth
of sun-split clouds—and done a hundred things
You have not dreamed of—wheeled and soared and swung
High in the sunlit silence. Hov'ring there,
I've chased the shouting wind along, and flung
My eager craft through footless halls of air.

Up, up the long, delirious, burning blue
I've topped the wind-swept heights with easy grace
Where never lark, or even eagle flew—

And, while the silent lifting mind I've trod
The high untrespassed sanctity of space,
Put out my hand and touched the face of God.

> *—John Gillespie Magee, Jr., RCAF (1922–1941). Read at
> teacher/astronaut Christa McAuliffe's funeral after her
> death in the 1986 Challenger space shuttle explosion.*

I Live for Thee

Home they brought her warrior dead;
She nor swoon'd nor utter'd cry.
All her maidens, watching, said,
She must weep or she will die.
Then they praised him, soft and low,
Call'd him worthy to be loved,
Truest friend and noblest foe;
Yet she neither spoke nor moved.
Stole a maiden from her place,
Lightly to the warrior stept,
Took the face-cloth from the face;
Yet she neither moved nor wept.
Rose a nurse of ninety years,
Set his child upon her knee—
Like summer tempest came her tears—
"Sweet my child, I live for thee."

> *—Alfred, Lord Tennyson (1809–1892)*

I'd Like to Think

I'd like to think when life is done
    That I had filled a needed post,
That here and there I'd paid my fare
    With more than idle talk and boast;
That I had taken gifts divine,
The breath of life and manhood fine,
And tried to use them now and then
In service for my fellow men.

> *—Edgar Albert Guest (1881–1959)*

The Lost Master

"And when I come to die," he said,
Ye shall not lay me out in state,
Nor leave your laurels at my head,
Nor cause your men of speech orate;
No monument your gift shall be,
No column in the Hall of Fame;
But just this line ye grave for me:
      'He played the game.'"

So when his glorious task was done,
It was not of his fame we thought;
It was not of his battles won,
But of the pride with which he fought;
But of his zest, his ringing laugh,
His trenchant scorn of praise or blame:
And so we graved his epitaph,
      "He played the game."

And so we, too, in humbler ways
Went forth to fight the fight anew,
And heeding neither blame nor praise,
We held the course he set us true.
And we, too, find the fighting sweet;
And we, too, fight for fighting's sake;
And though we go down in defeat,
And though our stormy hearts may break,
We will not do our Master shame:
We'll play the game, please God,
      We'll play the game.

      —*Robert W. Service (1874–1958)*

On a Dead Enemy

I came in haste with cursing breath,
    And heart of hardest steel;
But when I saw thee cold in death,
    I felt as man should feel.

For when I look upon that face,
    That cold, unheeding, frigid brow,
Where neither rage nor fear has place,
    By Heaven! I cannot hate thee now!

—Alfred, Lord Tennyson (1809–1892)

Requiem for One Slain in Battle

Breathe, trumpets, breathe
Slow notes of saddest wailing—
Sadly responsive peal, ye muffled drums;
Comrades, with downcast eyes
And banners trailing,
Attend him home,—
The youthful warrior comes.
Upon his shield,
Upon his shield returning,
Borne from the field of honor
Where he fell;
Glory and grief, together clasped
In mourning,
His fame, his fate
With sobs exulting tell.

Wrap round his breast,
The flag his breast defended—
His country's flag,
In battle's front unrolled:
For it he died;
On earth forever ended
His brave young life
Lives in each sacred fold.

With proud fond tears,
By tinge of shame untainted,
Bear him, and lay him
Gently in his grave:

Above the hero write,—
The young, half-sainted,—
His country asked his life,
His life he gave!

>   —*George Lunt (1803–1855)*

Youth in the Skies

These who were children yesterday
Now move in lovely flight,
Swift-glancing as the shooting stars
That cleave the summer night;

A moment flashed, they came and went,
Horizons rise and fall,
The speed of valour lifts them up
And strength obeys their call.

The downs below are breathing peace
With thyme and butterflies,
And sheep at pasture in the shade –
And now from English skies

Those who were children yesterday
Look down with other eyes;
Man's desperate folly was not there
But theirs the sacrifice.

Old men may wage a war of words,
Another race are these,
Who flash to glory dawn and night
Above the starry seas.

>   —*Herbert Asquith (1881–1947)*

CHAPTER EIGHT:
THE SPIRIT OF
LOVABLE LIFE
Tributes to Companion Animals and Pets

Beau by Loren Eiseley

Epitaph for a Cat by Margaret E. Bruner

Epitaph to a Dog by Lord George Gordon Byron

For a Dead Kitten by Sara Henderson Hay

Last Words to a Dumb Friend by Thomas Hardy

Missy 1966–1971 by Jim Harrison

An Obituary for a Dog by Warren G. Harding

One Small Furry Friend by Merrill O. Fisher

The Power of the Dog by Rudyard Kipling

Rainbow Bridge by Author Unknown

Rest in Peace by Dr. Wilfred John Funk

Tribute to the Memory of the Same Dog 1805. 1807 by William Wordsworth

How could this small body hold
So immense a thing as Death?
　　　　　—Sara Henderson Hay

A woman whose beloved Maltese had died declared that no one could possibly understand how bereft she felt with this loss. Yet she is not alone. Pet owners everywhere have experienced a cherished animal friend's death. To many, the loss haunts them still. One has only to visit the myriad Internet sites of pet memorials, virtual pet graveyards, and pet bereavement support networks to know how true this is. In our love for our pets, we almost choose to ignore the fact that they are decidedly shorter-lived than we are. We then learn to our sorrow that we must eventually watch them pass, bury them and somehow go on.

Elizabeth Whittemore's wonderful, touching poem *My Friends Are Little Lamps to Me*, found in Chapter Five, is one of the most appropriate readings for a companion animal's memorial service. Refer to that chapter for additional poems for friends, and also the general tributes located in Chapter Eleven.

Beau

Beau is gone now,
the huge black poodle
who, when I visited his owners,
always used to wave his yellow food dish
happily from the doorway and bark his welcome
or lie beside my bed in the morning.
This afternoon on the patio
his diminutive challenger the chipmunk
who used to set Beau wild
whistled dispute from the wall
but there was only silence.
I think even the chipmunk was abashed.
They had had a long rivalry and now silence
had fallen. A lily nodded gently
on its stem and I
went to my room where Beau
would never again turn three times around
and subside with a patient sigh while I wrote.
I am not a philosopher. I merely know
everything good has an end. I hope Beau
left without having learned this.
Yesterday his girl playmate from up the road
came by slowly, having come before.
How does one explain this to animals: that after a while
there are none of us left: no shadows, no voice, no odor.
One cannot even show a picture.
She goes away silently up the track.
She does not understand the world's absences.
Looking at the empty rug by my bed,
neither do I.

    —*Loren Eiseley (1907–1977)*

Epitaph for a Cat

If in some far-off, future day,
A stranger's feet should pass this way,
And if his gaze should seek the ground,
Wondering what lies beneath the mound:
Know that a cat of humble birth

Claims this small portion of the earth.
But I thought not of pedigree,
When, like a child, he came to me,—
A lonely waif, whose piteous cries
Were mirrored in his frightened eyes.
And so I beg that you will not
Defame or desecrate this spot
By ruthless act or idle jeer,
Though but a cat lies buried here.

—*Margaret E. Bruner (1886–1970?)*

Epitaph to a Dog

When some proud son of man returns to earth,
Unknown to glory, but upheld by birth,
The sculptor's art exhausts the pomp of woe,
And storied urns record who rests below;
When all is done, upon the tomb is seen,
Not what he was, but what he should have been.
But the poor dog, in life the firmest friend,
The first to welcome, foremost to defend,
Whose honest heart is still his master's own,
Who labors, fights, lives, breathes for him alone,
Unhonored falls, unnoticed all his worth,
Denied in heaven the soul held on earth —
while man, vain insect! hopes to be forgiven,
And claims himself a sole exclusive heaven.
Oh man! thou feeble tenant of an hour,
Debased by slavery, or corrupt by power —
Who knows thee well must quit thee with disgust,
Degraded mass of animated dust!
Thy love is lust, thy friendship all a cheat,
thy smiles hypocrisy, thy words deceit!
By nature vile, ennobled but by name,
Each kindred brute might bid thee blush for shame.
Ye, who perchance behold this simple urn,
Pass on — it honors none you wish to mourn.
To mark a friend's remains these stones arise;
I never knew but one — and there he lies.

—*Lord George Gordon Byron (1788–1824)*

For a Dead Kitten

Put the rubber mouse away,
Pick the spools up from the floor,
What was velvet-shod, and gay,
Will not want them any more.

What was warm, is strangely cold.
Whence dissolved the little breath?
How could this small body hold
So immense a thing as Death?

—*Sara Henderson Hay (1906–1987)*

Last Words to a Dumb Friend

Pet was never mourned as you,
Purrer of the spotless hue,
Plumy tail, and wistful gaze
While you humoured our queer ways,
Or outshrilled your morning call
Up the stairs and through the hall—
Foot suspended in its fall—
While, expectant, you would stand
Arched, to meet the stroking hand;
Till your way you chose to wend
Yonder, to your tragic end.

Never another pet for me!
Let your place all vacant be;
Better blankness day by day
Than companion torn away.
Better bid his memory fade,
Better blot each mark he made,
Selfishly escape distress
By contrived forgetfulness,
Than preserve his prints to make
Every morn and eve an ache.

From the chair whereon he sat
Sweep his fur, nor wince thereat;
Rake his little pathways out

Mid the bushes roundabout;
Smooth away his talon's mark
From the claw-worn pine-tree bark,
Where he climbed as dusk embrowned,
Waiting us who loitered round.

Strange it is this speechless thing,
Subject to our mastering,
Subject for his life and food
To our gift, and time, and mood;
Timid pensioner of us Powers,
His existence ruled by ours,
Should—by crossing at a breath
Into safe and shielded death,
By the merely taking hence
Of his insignificance—
Loom as largened to the sense,
Shape as part, above man's will,
Of the Imperturbable.

As a prisoner, flight debarred,
Exercising in a yard,
Still retain I, troubled, shaken,
Mean estate, by him forsaken;
And this home, which scarcely took
Impress from his little look,
By his faring to the Dim
Grows all eloquent of him.

Housemate, I can think you still
Bounding to the window-sill,
Over which I vaguely see
Your small mound beneath the tree,
Showing in the autumn shade
That you moulder where you played.

                    —*Thomas Hardy (1840–1928)*

Missy 1966–1971

I want to be worthy of this waking dream—
    floating   above
    the August landscape
in a coffin with my dog
who's just died from fibroid cancer.
Yes. We'll be up there and absorb
the light of stars and phosphorus
like the new Army telescopic sights
and the light hanging captive
in clouds
and the light glittering upward
from the water
and porchlights
from the few trucks & cars
at 3 A.M.
and one lone airliner.
Grief holding us safe in a knot we'll float
over every mile we covered, birch clump, thorn apple,
wild cherry trees and aspen in search of grouse,
your singular white figure fixed then as Sirius the Dog Star.
I think this crazed boy striking
out at nothing
wants to join you
so homeward
bound.

        —Jim Harrison (1937–)

An Obituary for a Dog

It isn't orthodox to ascribe a soul to a dog. But Hub was loving and loyal, with a jealousy that tests its quality. He was reverent, patient, faithful. He was sympathetic, more than humanly so sometimes, for no lure could be devised to call him from the sick bed of mistress or master. He minded his own affairs—especially worthy of human emulation. He was modest and submissive where these were becoming, yet he assumed a guardianship of the home he sentineled until entry was properly vouched. He couldn't speak our language, though he somehow understood. But he could be and was eloquent with uttering eye and wagging tail and the other expressions of knowing dogs. No, perhaps he had no soul, but in these things are the essence of soul and the spirit of loveable life.

Whether the Creator planned it so or environment and human companionship made it so, men may learn richly through the love and fidelity of a brave and devoted dog. Such loyalty might easily add luster to a crown of immortality.

—*Warren G. Harding (1865–1923)*

One Small Furry Friend

There was in our home, this small furry friend,
Who didn't ask to come into our lives,
Who didn't require much help or care.
Who didn't cost us anything, but a little food,
Who only asked for some of our love and attention.

This friend of ours didn't hurt anyone.
By thought or deed, he tried only to please.
All of our friend's life was spent
Trying to make us happy,
He asked for so little, but gave so much.
Never was he too tired, too hungry,
Never too sick to show us love.
In every way possible he demonstrated his love:
With the tilt of his head, the sparkle in his eye,
The wag of his tail.
How he waited for us to show him some attention,
So he could show us his love.
How he lived the golden rule!

This friend was one of our family,
A most important part of our lives.
He is sadly missed, but we are so much better,
For his having shared his life with us.
We can think of nothing, and perhaps
No one, that has better taught us
To give and receive love openly,
Unselfishly and unashamedly
As this one small furry friend.

—*Merrill O. Fisher*

The Power of the Dog

There is sorrow enough in the natural way
From men and women to fill our day;
And when we are certain of sorrow in store,
Why do we always arrange for more?
Brothers and sisters, I bid you beware
Of giving your heart to a dog to tear.
Buy a pup and your money will buy
Love unflinching that cannot lie—
Perfect passion and worship fed
By a kick in the ribs or a pat on the head.
Nevertheless it is hardly fair
To risk your heart to a dog to tear.

When the fourteen years which Nature permits
Are closing in asthma, or tumour, or fits,
And the vet's unspoken prescription runs
To lethal chambers or loaded guns,
Then you will find—it's your own affair—
But...you've given your heart to a dog to tear.

When the body that lived at your single will,
With its whimper of welcome, is stilled (how still!)
When the spirit that answered your every mood
Is gone—wherever it goes—for good,
You will discover how much you care,
And will give your heart to a dog to tear.

We've sorrow enough in the natural way,
When it comes to burying Christian clay.
Our lives are not given, but only lent,
At compound interest of cent per cent.
Though it is not always the case, I believe,
That the longer we've kept 'em, the more do we grieve:
For, when debts are payable, right or wrong,
A short-term loan is as bad as a long—
So why in—Heaven (before we are there)
Should we give our hearts to a dog to tear?

—Rudyard Kipling (1865–1936)

Rainbow Bridge

There is a bridge connecting Heaven and Earth. It is called the Rainbow Bridge because of its many colors. Just this side of the Rainbow Bridge, there is a land of meadows, hills and valleys, with lush green grass. When a beloved pet dies, the pet goes to this place. There is always food and water, and warm spring weather. Those old and frail animals are young again. Those who have been maimed are made whole again. They play all day with each other. There is only one thing missing. They are not with the special people who loved them on earth. So, each day they run and play until the day comes when one suddenly stops playing and looks up. The nose twitches, the ears are up, the eyes stare, and this one suddenly runs from the group. You have been seen, and when you and your special friend meet, you take him or her in your arms and embrace. Your face is kissed again and again and again, and you look once more into the eyes of your trusting pet. Then you cross the Rainbow Bridge together, never again to be separated.

—*Author Unknown*

Rest in Peace

Father, in Thy starry tent
I kneel, a humble suppliant...
A dog has died today on earth,
Of little worth
Yet very dear.
Gather him in Thine arms
If only
For a while.
I fear
He will be lonely...
Shield him with Thy smile.

—*Dr. Wilfred John Funk (1883–1965)*

**Tribute
to the Memory of the Same Dog
1805. 1807**

Lie here, without a record of thy worth,
Beneath a covering of the common earth!
It is not from unwillingness to praise,
Or want of love, that here no Stone we raise;
More thou deserv'st; but this man gives to man,
Brother to brother, this is all we can.
Yet they to whom thy virtues made thee dear
Shall find thee through all changes of the year:
This Oak points out thy grave; the silent tree
Will gladly stand a monument of thee.
     We grieved for thee, and wished thy end were past;
And willingly have laid thee here at last:
For thou hadst lived till everything that cheers
In thee had yielded to the weight of years;
Extreme old age had wasted thee away,
And left thee but a glimmering of the day:
Thy ears were deaf, and feeble were thy knees—
I saw thee stagger in the summer breeze,
Too weak to stand against its sportive breath,
And ready for the gentlest stroke of death.
It came, and we were glad; yet tears were shed;
Both man and woman wept when thou wert dead;
Not only for a thousand thoughts that were,
Old household thoughts, in which thou hadst thy share;
But for some precious boons vouchsafed to thee,
Found scarcely anywhere in like degree!
For love, that comes wherever life and sense
Are given by God, in thee was most intense;
A chain of heart, a feeling of the mind,
A tender sympathy, which did thee bind
Not only to us Men, but to thy Kind:
Yea, for thy fellow-brutes in thee we saw
A soul of love, love's intellectual law:—
Hence, if we wept, it was not done in shame;
Our tears from passion and from reason came,
And, therefore, shalt thou be an honoured name!

   —William Wordsworth (1770–1850)

CHAPTER NINE:
BECAUSE HE LIVED
Tributes to Men

This his success, that at the end
Men mourned the passing of a friend.
—Edgar Albert Guest

It is not easy choosing words to acknowledge the life, and death, of a man. Somehow, it is more readily acceptable in society to speak of the love and intimacy of a relationship with a woman than with a man, whether he was father or son, grandfather or uncle, student or teacher, colleague or associate, brother, friend or lover. It may seem as though it is only a wife who is permitted to talk of her partner with deep emotion or a profound sense of loss. And so everyone else is left bereft of both the words and the friend.

Authors have dealt with this dilemma—of reaching for an expression appropriate for the solemn occasion, that will honor the man who has died and not embarrass the writer with flowery prose or weepy words—by writing tributes infused with dignity and honor. Several of the poems selected for this section will be instantly familiar. "He has achieved success who has lived well" from *What Is Success?* by Bessie Anderson Stanley and *The Gentle Man* by Edgar Albert Guest are examples of tribute readings that speak of high regard and great loss. These compositions demonstrate that a man can still be much cherished and missed, with a testimonial that both respects and mourns him.

Chapter Five (friends) and Chapter Eleven (general tributes) are other options for appropriate selections. The well-known verse "Home is the sailor, home from the sea" from *Requiem* by Robert Louis Stevenson, found in Chapter Two (fathers), is another possibility. For more passionate remembrances, see Chapter Four (tributes to soul mates, spouses and lovers).

Epilogue

He died in December. He must descend
Somewhere, vague and cold, the spirit and seal.
Somewhere. Imagination one's one friend
Cannot see there. Both of us at the end.
Nouns, verbs do not exist for what I feel.

—John Berryman (1914–1972)

Epitaph

Having lived long in time,
He lives now in timelessness
Without sorrow, made perfect
By our never finished love,
By our compassion and forgiveness,
And by his happiness in receiving
These gifts we give. Here in time
We are added to one another forever.

—Wendell Berry (1934–)

Eulogy for a Bachelor
Dedicated to Gary Slesinger 1953–1994

Nothing will stop. Nothing deter its course.
Yet this empty void will remain unfilled,
in all the lives he touched with this shyest
nature, which concealed such real potential.

Shock halts us leaden in our heavy steps
at the abrupt loss of his widest smile,
which leaves the brilliance of the sun covered
by a haze as his lasting legacy.

Parental strength was there for this loved man.
Don't be saddened by what you wished for him.
No more will he suffer pangs of sorrow.
Nor endure others' perpetrated hurts.

Soft and kind were his characteristics,
so precious in the brashness of our days.
Plead that all other egos could be this
well restrained. Surely then strife should cease.

      —Leslie Fine (1925–)

The Gentle Man

His life was gentle, and his mind
The little splendors seemed to find.
      The baser side of life he saw,
      But from the blemish and the flaw
He turned, as if he understood
That none of us is wholly good.

He lived as one who seemed to know
That as the swift days come and go
      Clouds blanket skies that should be fair,
      Rain is encountered everywhere,
And so o'er every human form
Must blow at times the bitter storm.

As one who loves a garden, he
Walked round the world its charms to see.
      Not only by the rose he stayed,
      The tiniest violet in the shade
On his devotion could depend,
To great and low he played the friend.

And as the gardener seems to give
More care to plants which fight to live
      So he, with tenderer regard,
      Befriended those whose tasks were hard.
Thus dealing gently, he became
More than a high and haughty name.

This was his wealth, that good and bad
Of him some happy memory had.
      This was his fame, that high and low

Their love for him were proud to show.
This his success, that at the end
Men mourned the passing of a friend.

—*Edgar Albert Guest (1881–1959)*

In Memoriam

Look, till all of his years,
Foreshortened in your gaze,
Become, as under glass,
A few intensest days.

See? The courageous head—
The brown one—the white—
It flickers like a single
Star in densest night.

Listen. But no sound.
Not even glancing here.
The fever in him flashes:
The love against the fear.

Anxiety in this man
Yet could not kill the heart,
That now is burning coal,
And his immensest part.

The panic, the distress—
Oh, brothers, do not cry.
His love alone is climbing
The fences of the sky.

—*Mark Van Doren (1894–1973)*

Let Me Go Down to Dust

Let me go down to dust and dreams
Gently, O Lord, with never a fear
Of death beyond the day that is done;
In such a manner as beseems
A kinsman of the wild, a son
Of stoic earth whose race is run.

Let me go down as any deer,
Who, broken by a desperate flight,
Sinks down to slumber for the night—
Dumbly serene in certitude
That it will rise again at dawn,
Buoyant, refreshed of limb, renewed,
And confident that it will thrill
To-morrow to its nuzzling fawn,
To the bugle-notes of elk upon the hill.

Let me go down to dreams and dust
Gently, O Lord, with quiet trust
And the fortitude that marks a child
Of earth, a kinsman of the wild.
Let me go down as any doe
That nods upon its ferny bed
And, lulled to slumber by the flow
Of talking water, the muffled brawl
Of far cascading waterfall,
At last lets down its weary head
Deep in the brookments in the glen;
And under the starry-candled sky,
With never the shadow of a sigh,
Gives its worn body back to earth again.

　　　—Lew Sarett (1888–1954)

The Man Has Spread His Silver Wings

The man has spread his silver wings,
Is six miles nearer heaven,
Has climbed the tumbleweed of cloud,
Conquers where no bird has striven;
His wings wink joy before his breeze,
His pockets billow and let loose the sky,
Two streaming trails, the fountains of his play,
Lie smoking on, though he has catapulted by.

　　　—Elizabeth Aldrich

Oh, Breathe Not His Name

Oh, breathe not his name! Let it sleep in the shade,
Where cold and unhonored his relics are laid;
Sad, silent, and dark be the tears that we shed,
As the night-dew that falls on the grass o'er his head.

But the night-dew that falls, though in silence it weeps,
Shall brighten with verdure the grave where he sleeps;
And the tear that we shed, though in secret it rolls,
Shall long keep his memory green in our souls.

—*Thomas Moore (1779–1852)*

People Liked Him

People liked him, not because
        He was rich or known to fame;
He had never won applause
        As a star in any game.
His was not a brilliant style,
        His was not a forceful way,
But he had a gentle smile
        And a kindly word to say.

Never arrogant or proud,
        On he went with manner mild;
Never quarrelsome or loud,
        Just as simple as a child;
Honest, patient, brave and true;
        Thus he lived from day to day,
Doing what he found to do
        In a cheerful sort of way.

Wasn't one to boast of gold
        Or belittle it with sneers,
Didn't change from hot to cold,
        Kept his friends throughout the years,
Sort of man you like to meet
        Any time or any place.
There was always something sweet
        And refreshing in his face.

Sort of man you'd like to be:
> Balanced well and truly square;
Patient in adversity,
> Generous when skies were fair.
Never lied to friend or foe,
> Never rash in word or deed,
Quick to come and slow to go
> In a neighbor's time of need.

Never rose to wealth or fame,
> Simply lived, and simply died,
But the passing of his name
> Left a sorrow, far and wide.
Not for glory he'd attained,
> Nor for what he had of pelf,
Were the friends that he had gained,
> But for what he was himself.

> —*Edgar Albert Guest (1881–1959)*

Sail On, Sail On

Sail on, sail on, thou fearless bark—
Wherever blows the welcome wind,
It cannot lead to scenes more dark,
More sad, than those we leave behind.
Each wave that passes seems to say,
Though death beneath our smile may be,
Less cold we are, less false than they
Whose smiling wrecked thy hopes and thee.

Sail on, sail on—through endless space—
Through calm—through tempest—stop no more;
The stormiest sea's a resting-place
To him who leaves such hearts on shore.
Or—if some desert land we met,
Where never yet false-hearted men
Profaned a world that else were sweet—
Then rest thee, bark, but not till then.

> —*Thomas Moore (1779–1852)*

What Are Years?

What is our innocence,
what is our guilt? All are
naked, none is safe. And whence
is courage: the unanswered question,
the resolute doubt—
dumbly calling, deadly listening—that
is misfortune, even death,
encourages others
and in its defeat, stirs

the soul to be strong? He
sees deep and is glad, who
accedes to mortality
and in his imprisonment rises
upon himself as
the sea in a chasm, struggling to be
free and unable to be,
in its surrendering
finds its continuing.

So he who strongly feels,
behaves. The very bird,
grown taller as he sings, steels
his form straight up. Though he is captive,
his mighty singing
says, satisfaction is a lowly
thing, how pure a thing is joy.
This is mortality,
this is eternity.

—Marianne Moore (1887–1972)

What Is Success?

He has achieved success who has lived well, laughed often, and loved
much; who has enjoyed the trust of pure women, the respect of intel-
ligent men, and the love of little children; who has filled his niche and
accomplished his task; who has left the world better than he found it,
whether by an improved poppy, a perfect poem, or a rescued soul; who

has never lacked appreciation of earth's beauty or failed to express it; who has always looked for the best in others and given the best he had; whose life was an inspiration and whose memory a benediction.

—Bessie Anderson Stanley

CHAPTER TEN:
WOMAN MUCH MISSED
Tributes to Women

She who lived valiantly has passed,
Why should we grieve,
Why should it break our hearts like this
If we believe?
—Grace Noll Crowell

A tribute to a much beloved woman can be as lengthy and noble as *Elegy* by Lucy Harrington or as simple and eloquent as Jan Struther's *Biography*.

A woman can be a mother, daughter, sister, lover, friend, or the complex and satisfying mesh of friend *and* mother, friend *and* sister, friend *and* daughter, friend *and* lover. How fortunate to have experienced a relationship with a woman in more than one dimension. For this reason, it is essential to refer to the chapters on friends (Chapter Five), lovers (Chapter Four), siblings (Chapter Six), mothers (Chapter One), or general tributes (Chapter Eleven), to see if there is a poem that closely matches the depth and breadth of the person and relationship to be honored.

Biography

One day my life will end, and lest
Some whim should prompt you to review it,
Let her who knows the subject best
Tell the shortest way to do it.
Then say: "Here lies one doubly blest."
Say: "She was happy." Say: "She knew it."

—Jan Struther (1901–1953)

A Death-Bed

Her suffering ended with the day,
Yet lived she at its close,
And breathed the long, long night away
In statue-like repose.

But when the sun in all his state
Illumed the eastern skies,
She passed through Glory's morning gate
And walked in Paradise!

—James Aldrich (1810–1956)

Elegy

Death be not proud, thy hand gave not this blow,
Sin was her captive, whence thy power doth flow;
The executioner of wrath thou art,
But to destroy the just is not thy part.
Thy coming, terror, anguish, grief denounce;
Her happy state, courage, ease, joy pronounce.
From out the crystal palace of her breast,
The clearer soul was called to endless rest,
(Not by the thundering voice, wherewith God threats,
But, as with crowned saints in heaven he treats)
And, waited on by angels, home was brought,
To joy that it through many dangers sought;
The key of mercy gently did unlock
The doors twixt heaven and it, when life did knock.

Nor boast, the fairest frame was made thy prey,
Because to mortal eyes it did decay;
A better witness than thou art, assures,
That though dissolved, it yet a speck endures;
No dram thereof shall want or loss sustain,
When her best soul inhabits it again.
Go then to people cursed before they were,
Their spoils in triumph of thy conquest wear.
Glory not though thy self in these hot tears
Which our face, not for hers, but our harm wears,
The mourning livery given by Grace, not thee,
Which wills our souls in these streams washed should be,
And on our hearts, her memory's best tomb,
In this her epitaph doth write thy doom.
Blind were those eyes, saw not how bright did shine
Through flesh's misty veil the beams divine.
Deaf were the ears, not charmed with that sweet sound
Which did in the spirit-instructed voice abound.
Of flint the conscience, did not yield and melt,
At what in her last Act it saw, heard, felt.
Weep not, nor grudge then, to have lost her sight,
Taught thus, our after stay's but a short night:
But by all souls not by corruption choked
Let in high raised notes that power be invoked.
Calm the rough seas, by which she sails to rest,
From sorrows here, to a kingdom ever blest;
And teach this hymn of her with joy, and sing.
The grave no conquest gets, Death hath no sting.

—Lucy Harrington, Countess of Bedford (died 1627)

Of One Who Lived Valiantly

She who lived valiantly has passed,
Why should we grieve,
Why should it break our hearts like this
If we believe?

Surely she lives more valiantly
Than ever before,
Freed, as she is, to move without
The weights she bore;

Freed for the sweet adventurings
Of heavenly days,
Lightened, to go exploring down
The glory-ways.

What must these first hours be to her
Who loved earth so?
How swift, how very swift and glad
Her feet must go!

She who lived valiantly has passed,
Who should we grieve?
Why should it break our hearts like this
If we believe?

—Grace Noll Crowell (1877–?)

A Perfect Woman

A perfect Woman, nobly planned
To warn, to comfort and command,
And yet a Spirit still, and bright
With something of angelic light.

> *—William Wordsworth (1770–1850). Excerpted from "She Was a Phantom of Delight." Found on a handwritten note tacked to the gate of Kensington Palace, after the 1997 death of Diana, Princess of Wales.*

The Rose Still Grows Beyond the Wall

Near a shady wall a rose once grew,
Budded and blossomed in God's free light,
Watered and fed by morning dew,
Shedding its sweetness day and night.

As it grew and blossomed fair and tall,
Slowly rising to loftier height,
It came to a crevice in the wall,
Through which there shone a beam of light.

Onward it crept with added strength,
With never a thought of fear or pride.

It followed the light through the crevice's length
And unfolded itself on the other side.

The light, the dew, the broadening view
Were found the same as they were before;
And it lost itself in beauties new,
Breathing its fragrance more and more.

Small claims of death cause us to grieve,
And makes our courage faint or fail?
Nay! Let us faith and hope received:
The rose still grows beyond the wall.

Scattering fragrance far and wide,
Just as it did in days of yore,
Just as it did on the other side,
Just as it will forevermore.

> —*Almira L. Frink (1870–?)*

Sonnet XII

When I do count the clock that tells the time,
And see the brave day sunk in hideous night;
When I behold the violet past prime,
And sable curls all silver'd o'er with white;
When lofty trees I see barren of leaves,
Which erst from heat did canopy the herd,
And summer's green all girded up in sheaves
Born on the bier with white and bristly beard;
Then of thy beauty do I question make
That thou among the wastes of time must go,
Since sweets and beauties do themselves forsake,
And die as fast as they see others grow;
       And nothing gainst Time's scythe can make defence
       Save breed, to brave him when he takes thee hence.

> —*William Shakespeare (1564–1616)*

Vanishment (for Rose)

I remember a woman
who stood up from her chair
and painted life's images
in bold colors of earth and sky.
Then sat down to write
of the people with whom
she equated as earthlings,
glad for herself
and self contained.

Nothing awakens her.
I look on to watch losing myself
in memory of a woman to whom
love was meaning, leaving me
stranded in my own vanishment
from the life we led together
hand in hand
lip to lip.

—David Ignatow (1914–1997)

The Voice

Woman much missed, how you call to me, call to me,
Saying that now you are not as you were
When you had changed from the one who was all to me,
But as at first, when our day was fair.

Can it be you that I hear? Let me view you, then,
Standing as when I drew near to the town
Where you would wait for me: yes, as I knew you then,
Even to the original air-blue gown!

Or is it only the breeze, in its listlessness
Travelling across the wet mead to me here,
You being ever dissolved to wan wistlessness,
Heard no more again far or near?

Thus I; faltering forward,
Leaves around me falling,
Wind oozing thin through the thorn from norward,
And the woman calling.

>   *—Thomas Hardy (1840–1928)*

While Weeping Friends

While weeping friends bend over the silent tomb
Recount her Virtues and their loss deplore
Faiths piercing eyes dart thro' the dreary gloom
and hail her blest: where tears shall flow no more.

>   *—Author Unknown. From the 1794 gravestone of Ann*
>   *Barbara Bender in the Granary Burying Ground, Boston,*
>   *Massachusetts.*

CHAPTER ELEVEN:
I CANNOT FORGET YOU
General Tributes

All the Wisdom by Odell Shepard

The Appeal by Rudyard Kipling

Ascension by Colleen Corah Hitchcock

Be Still My Soul by Katharina von Schlege

Bound by Theodore Roethke

The Chambered Nautilus by Oliver Wendell Holmes

The Choir Invisible by George Eliot

A Clown's Prayer by Author Unknown

Courage by Amelia Earhart

Cover Me Over by Richard Eberhart

Dear Sam by Laurie Colwin

Death, Be Not Proud Holy Sonnet X by John Donne

Divine Child Rolls On by Nancy Willard

Do Not Weep for Me by Author Unknown

Elegy Written in a Country Churchyard by Thomas Gray

The Exequies by Thomas Stanley

Farewell, My Friends by Clarence Day

For Katrina's Sun Dial by Henry van Dyke

Gather the Stars by Carl Sandburg

Give Me My Scallop-Shell of Quiet by Sir Walter Alexander Raleigh

God Saw You Getting Tired by Author Unknown

A Good-night by Francis Quarles

Grieve Not for Beauty by Witter Bynner

I Cannot Forget You translated from the Maka

I Think Continually of Those Who Were Truly Great by Stephen Spender

If You Come Softly by Audre Lorde

Immortality by Mary E. Frye

In Memoriam by Gordon Parks

In the Garden of Dreams by Louise Chandler Moulton

In This Short Life by Emily Dickinson

Ithaka by Constantine P. Cavafy

A Little Work by George Louis P.B. DuMaurier

Miss Me—But Let Me Go by Edgar Albert Guest

No Coward Soul by Emily Brontë

Pleas by Leslie Fine

Reading from Henry Scott Holland (1847–1918) Canon of St. Paul's Cathedral by Author Unknown

A Reason for Life by Shelby M. Forrest

Song of the River by William Randolph Hearst

Swiftly Beyond Our Measure by Author Unknown

There Is No Death by Author Unknown

They Are Not Long by Ernest Dowson

Tichborne's Elegy by Chidiock Tichborn

To a Seaman Dead on Land by Kay Boyle

To Night by Joseph Blanco White

To Those I Love by Isla Paschal Richardson

To Virgins, to Make Much of Time by Robert Herrick

Turn Again to Life by Mary Lee Hall

Undo It, Take It Back by Nessa Rapoport

When I Am Gone by Author Unknown

When I Die by Author Unknown

Yes Thou Art Gone by Anne Brontë

Love doesn't die,
People do.
—Author Unknown

The readings found in this chapter have universal appeal. They are not specific to gender, age or relationship. The subject is often "you" or "one" or "thou"; often the reading is narrated from the first person standpoint of "I" or "my."

These selections were chosen because they can be read out loud without sounding stilted or overly "rhyme-y." There are more than 50 readings here, in alphabetical order by title.

What are you looking for in a memorial reading or poem? For some people, the most important attribute of the poem is that it is short. If this describes your needs, read *Cover Me Over; Dear Sam; Divine Child Rolls On; For Katrina's Sun Dial; I Cannot Forget You;* and *In This Short Life.* These readings say much in a very few words.

Some people feel uncomfortable having to say anything flowery or emotional. For those who just want to say goodbye in a quiet and dignified manner, *All the Wisdom, Even Such Is Time* and *I'd Like to Think* can be read without embarrassment by just about anyone.

Look over the readings in this section. If you do not find what you want here, find the section of the book that most closely resembles your relationship with the deceased, and work from there.

All the Wisdom

All the wisdom, all the beauty, I have lived for unaware
Came upon me by the rote of highland rills;
I have seen God walking there
In the solemn soundless air
When the morning wakened wonder in the hills.
"Let me sleep among the shadows of the mountains when I die."

—Odell Shepard (1884–1967)

The Appeal

If I have given you delight
   By aught that I have done,
Let me lie quiet in that night
   Which shall be yours anon:
And for the little, little, span
   The dead are borne in mind,
Seek not to question other than
   The books I leave behind.

—Rudyard Kipling (1865–1936)

Ascension

And if I go,
while you're still here...
Know that I live on,
vibrating to a different measure
—behind a veil you cannot see through.
You will not see me,
so you must have faith.
I wait for the time when we can soar together again
—both aware of each other.
Until then, live your life to its fullest and when you need me,
Just whisper my name in your heart
...I will be there.

—Colleen Corah Hitchcock. Appears in the front of Tom Clancy's book Without Remorse.

Be Still My Soul

Be still my soul: the Lord is on thy side;
Bear patiently the cross of grief or pain;
Leave to thy God to order and provide;
In very change He faithful will remain.
Be still, my soul; thy best, thy heav'nly Friend
Thro' thorny ways leads to a joyful end.

Be still, my soul: thy God doth undertake
To guide the future as He has the past.
Thy hope, thy confidence let nothing shake;
All now mysterious shall be bright at last.
Be still my soul: the waves and winds still know
His voice who ruled them while He dwelt below.

Be still, my soul: the hour is hastn'ning on
When we shall be forever with the Lord,
When disappointment, grief, and fear are gone,
Sorrow forgot, love's purest joys restored.
Be still my soul: when change and tears are past,
All safe and blessed we shall meet at last.

> —*Katharina von Schlege (1752). Read at a funeral in the novel* Cold Sassy Tree *by Olive Ann Burns (Ticknor & Fields, 1984).*

Bound

Negative tree, you are belief
Engendered by an iron grief,

A variously compounded fact
Denied the favor of swift act.

With terrible precision, you
Can split the aging rock in two;

Yet in your dumb profusion there
Is quiet, positive and clear.

You are a timeless sorrow thrust
Beyond the dreamlessness of dust.

You are a bird, securely bound,
That sings the song of voiceless ground,

And builds a nest in sterile stone,
Yet breeds no kin of flesh and bone.
You are a bird denied, the blood
Of earth in flying attitude.

—Theodore Roethke (1908–1963)

The Chambered Nautilus

This is the ship of pearl, which, poets feign,
        Sails the unshadowed main—
        The venturous bark that flings
On the sweet summer wind its purpled wings
In gulfs enchanted, where the Siren sings,
        And coral reefs lie bare,
Where the cold sea-maids rise to sun their streaming hair.

Its webs of living gauze no more unfurl!
        Wrecked is the ship of pearl!
        And every chambered cell,
Where its dim dreaming life was wont to dwell,
As the frail tenant shaped his growing shell,
        Before thee lies revealed—
Its irised ceiling rent, its sunless crypt unsealed!

Year after year beheld the silent toil
        That spread his lustrous coil;
        Still as the spiral grew,
He left the past year's dwelling for the new,
Stole with soft step its shining archway through,
        Built up its idle door,
Stretched in his last-found home, and knew the old no more.

Thanks for the heavenly message brought by thee,
        Child of the wandering sea,
        Cast from her lap forlorn!
From thy dead lips a clearer note is born
Than ever Triton blew from wreathed horn!
        While on mine ear it rings,
Through the deep caves of thought I hear a voice that sings:—

Build thee more stately mansions, O my soul,
    As the swift seasons roll!
    Leave thy low-vaulted past!
Let each new temple, nobler than the last,
Shut thee from heaven with a dome more vast,
    Till thou at length are free,
Leaving thine outgrown shell by life's unresting sea!

—Oliver Wendell Holmes (1809–1894)

The Choir Invisible

Oh, may I join the choir invisible
Of those immortal dead who live again
In minds made better by their presence; live
In pulses stirred to generosity,
In deeds of daring rectitude, in scorn
For miserable aims that end with self,
In thoughts sublime that pierce the night like stars,
And with their mild persistence urge men's search
To vaster issues. So to live is heaven:
To make undying music in the world,
Breathing a beauteous order that controls
With growing sway the growing life of man.
So we inherit that sweet purity
For which we struggled, failed, and agonized
With widening retrospect that bred despair.
Rebellious flesh that would not be subdued,
A vicious parent shaming still its child,
Poor anxious penitence, is quick dissolved;
Its discords, quenched by meeting harmonies,
Die in the large and charitable air,
And all our rarer, better, truer self
That sobbed religiously in yearning song,
That watched to ease the burden of the world,
Laboriously tracing what must be,
And what may yet be better—saw within
A worthier image for the sanctuary,
And shaped it forth before the multitude,
Divinely human, raising worship so

To higher reverence more mixed with love—
That better self shall live till human Time
Shall fold its eyelids, and the human sky
Be gathered like a scroll within the tomb
Unread forever. This is life to come—
Which martyred men have made more glorious
For us who strive to follow. May I reach
That purest heaven—be to other souls
The cup of strength in some great agony,
Enkindle generous ardor, feed pure love,
Beget the smiles that have no cruelty,
Be the sweet presence of a good diffused,
And in diffusion ever more intense!
So shall I join the choir invisible
Whose music is the gladness of the world.

> —*George Eliot (Marian Evans Cross) (1819–1880)*

A Clown's Prayer

As I stumble through this life
Help me to create more laughter than tears,
Dispense more happiness than gloom,
Spread more cheer than despair.
Never let me grow so big that I will fail to see
The wonder in the eyes of a child
Or the twinkle in the eyes of the aged.
Never let me forget that my total effort is to cheer people,
Make them happy,
And make them forget at least momentarily
All the unpleasant things in their lives.
And, in my final moment,
May I hear You whisper:
"When you made My people smile,
You made Me smile."

> —*Author Unknown. Given as a tribute at the 1997 funeral of
> comedian Christopher Farley.*

Courage

Courage is the price that life exacts for granting peace
The soul that knows it not, knows no release
From little things knows not the livid loneliness of fear

Nor mountain heights where bitter joy can
Hear the sound of wings.
How can life grant us boon of living, compensate

For dull gray ugliness and pregnant hate
Unless we dare
The soul's dominion? Each time we make a choice, we pay

With courage to behold resistless day
And count it fair.

—Amelia Earhart (1897–1937)

Cover Me Over

Cover me over, clover;
Cover me over, grass.
The mellow day is over
And there is night to pass.

Green arms about my head,
Green fingers on my hands.
Earth has no quieter bed
In all her quiet lands.

—Richard Eberhart (1904–)

Dear Sam

Dear Sam, your presence taught us fleetness, the joy of being mobile.
Let us not ponder what could have been, but try to rejoice in what was.
May we all learn from your life the sweetness and glory of a passionate spirit and may we think of you when our courage falters. May God
bless you and keep you.

—Laurie Colwin (1944–1992)

Death, Be Not Proud
Holy Sonnet X

Death, be not proud, though some have called thee
Mighty and dreadful, for thou art not so;
For those whom thou think'st thou dost overthrow
Die not, poor Death, nor yet canst thou kill me.
From rest and sleep, which but thy pictures be,
Much pleasure; then from thee much more must flow,
And soonest our best men with thee do go,
Rest of their bones, and soul's delivery.
Thou'rt slave to fate, chance, kings, and desperate men,
And dost with poison, war, and sickness dwell;
And poppy or charms can make us sleep as well
And better than thy stroke; why swell'st thou then?
One short sleep past, we wake eternally,
And death shall be no more: Death, thou shalt die.

—John Donne (1572–1631)

Divine Child Rolls On

Lullaby, my sparrow.
Cipher, make your mark
in the Book of Being.
Fly into the dark,

passenger of the planet.
Sun and stars are gone.
The Divine Child find you,
bless you, and roll on.

—Nancy Willard (1936–)

Do Not Weep for Me

Do not weep for me, for I have lived...
I have joined my hand with my fellows' hands,
to leave the planet better than I found it.

Do not weep for me, for I have loved and been loved by
my family, by those I loved who loved me back.
For I never knew a stranger, only friends.

Do not weep for me.
When you feel the ocean spray upon your face,
I am there.
When your heart beats faster at the dolphin's leaping grace,
I am there.
When you reach out to touch another's heart,
as now I touch God's face,
I am there.
Do not weep for me. I am not gone.

> *—Author Unknown. Recited at the 1991 funeral of actor Michael Landon.*

From Elegy Written in a Country Churchyard

Let not Ambition mock their useful toil,
    Their homely joys, and destiny obscure;
Nor Grandeur bear with a disdainful smile
    The short and simple annals of the poor.

Full many a gem of purest ray serene,
    The dark unfathom'd caves of ocean bear:
Full many a flower is born to blush unseen,
    And waste its sweetness on the desert air.

> *—Thomas Gray (1716–1771)*

The Exequies

Draw near
You Lovers that complain
Of Fortune or Disdain,
And to my Ashes lend a tear;
Melt the hard marble with your grones,
And soften the relentless Stones,
Whose cold imbraces the sad Subject hide
Of all Loves cruelties, and Beauties Pride.

No Verse
No Epicedium bring,
Nor peaceful Requiem sing,
To charm the terrours of my Herse;

No prophane Numbers must flow neer
The sacred silence that dwells here;
Vast Griefs are dumb, softly, oh softly mourn
Lest you disturb the Peace attends my Urn.
Yet strew
Upon my dismall Grave,
Such offerings as you have,
Forsaken Cypresse and sad Ewe;
For kinder Flowers can take no Birth
Or growth from such unhappy Earth.
Weep only o're my Dust, and say, Here lies
To Love and Fate an equal Sacrifice.

> —*Thomas Stanley (1625–1678)*

Farewell, My Friends

Farewell, my friends –farewell and hail!
I'm off to seek the Holy Grail.
        I cannot tell you why.

Remember, please, when I am gone,
'Twas Aspiration led me on.
Tiddely-widdlely tootle-oo
All I want is to stay with you.
        But here I go. Goodbye.

> —*Clarence Day (1874–1935). Recited by Charles Kuralt*
> *upon retiring from the TV program* Good Morning Sunday.

For Katrina's Sun Dial

Time is too slow for those who wait,
Too swift for those who fear,
Too long for those who grieve,
Too short for those who rejoice,
But for those who love, time is
Eternity.

> —*Henry van Dyke (1852–1933). Read by Lady Jane*
> *Fellowes at the 1997 funeral of Princess Diana.*

Gather the Stars

Gather the stars if you wish it so
Gather the songs and keep them.
Gather the faces of women.
Gather for keeping years and years.
And then...
Loosen your hands, let go and say good-bye.
Let the stars and songs go.
Let the faces and years go.
Loosen your hands and say good-bye.

—Carl Sandburg (1878–1967)

Give Me My Scallop-Shell of Quiet

Give me my scallop-shell of quiet,
My staff of faith to walk upon,
My scrip of joy, immortal diet,
My bottle of salvation,
My gown of glory, hope's true gauge;
And thus I'll take my pilgrimage.

—Sir Walter Alexander Raleigh (1861–1922)

God Saw You Getting Tired

God saw you getting tired,
When a cure was not to be.
So He wrapped his arms around you,
and whispered, "Come to me."

You didn't deserve what you went through,
So He gave you rest.
God's garden must be beautiful,
He only takes the best

And when I saw you sleeping,
So peaceful and free from pain
I could not wish you back
To suffer that again.

—Author Unknown

A Good-night

Close now thine eyes and rest secure;
Thy soul is safe enough, thy body sure;
   He that loves thee, He that keeps
And guards thee, never slumbers, never sleeps.

The smiling conscience in a sleeping breast
   Has only peace, has only rest;
   The music and the mirth of kings
Are all but very discords, when she sings;
   Then close thine eyes and rest secure;
No sleep so sweet as thine, no rest so sure.

       —Francis Quarles (1592–1644)

Grieve Not for Beauty

Grieve not for the invisible, transported brow
On which like leaves the dark hair grew,
Nor for the lips of laughter that are now
Laughing inaudibly in sun and dew,
Nor for those limbs that, fallen low
And seeming faint and slow,
Shall yet pursue
More ways of swiftness than the swallow dips
Among…and find more winds than ever blew
The straining sails of unimpeded ships!
Mourn not!—yield only happy tears
To deeper beauty than appears!

       —Witter Bynner (1881–1977)

I Cannot Forget You

No matter how hard I try to forget you, you always come back
    to my thoughts.
When you hear me singing I am really crying for you.

       —Translated from the Maka (1939)

I Think Continually of Those Who Were Truly Great

I think continually of those who are truly great.
Who from the womb, remembered the soul's history
Through corridors of light where the hours are suns,
Endless and singing. Whose lovely ambition
Was that their lips, still touched with fire,
Should tell of the spirit clothed from head to foot in sun.
And who hoarded from the spring branches
The desires falling across their bodies like blossoms.

What is precious is never to forget
The delight of the blood drawn from ageless springs
Breaking through rocks in worlds before our earth;
Never to deny its pleasure in the simple morning light,
Nor its grave evening demand for love;
Never to allow gradually the traffic to smother
With noise and fog the flowering of the spirit.
Near the snow, near the sun, in the highest fields
See how those names are feted by the wavering grass,
And by the streamers of white cloud,
And whispers of wind in the listening sky;
The names of those who in their lives fought for life,
Who wore at their hearts the fire's centre.
Borne of the sun they traveled a short while toward the sun,
And left the vivid air signed with their honour.

> —*Sir Stephen Spender (1909–1995). Read by President Bill Clinton at the 1996 funeral of Congresswoman Barbara Jordan.*

If You Come Softly

If you come as softly
As wind within the trees
You may hear what I hear
See what sorrow sees.

If you come as lightly
As threading dew
I will take you gladly
Nor ask more of you.

You may sit beside me
Silent as a breath
Only those who stay dead
Shall remember death.

And if you come I will be silent
Nor speak harsh words to you.
I will not ask you why, now.
Or how, or what you do.

We shall sit here, softly
Beneath two different years
And the rich earth between us
Shall drink our tears.

> —*Audre Lorde (1934–1992)*

Immortality

Do not stand at my grave and weep;
I am not there. I do not sleep.
I am a thousand winds that blow;
I am diamond glints of snow;
I am the sunlight on ripened grain;
I am the gentle autumn's rain.
When you awaken in the morning's hush;
I am the swift uplifting rush
of quiet birds' encircled flight.
I am the soft star that shines at night.
Do not stand at my grave and cry;
I am not there, I did not die.

> —*Mary E. Frye. Read at the funerals of Howard Hawks
> (1977) and Nicole Brown Simpson(1994). Recited in the
> 1978 TV movie* Better Late Than Never *and the 1996 TV
> movie* Dalva.

In Memoriam (for Moneta Sleet)

Your silence won't separate you from us,
nor from the hope you spawned—
particularly during those ungentle hours

when many black hearts seemed stripped of hope.
Best now that each of us attempt
to keep growing as you grew...

> —*Gordon Parks (1912–)*

In the Garden of Dreams
Louisa M. Alcott
In Memoriam

As the wind at play with a spark
Of fire that glows through the night;
As the speed of the soaring lark
That wings to the sky his flight;
So swiftly thy soul has sped
On its upward, wonderful way,
Like the lark, when the dawn is red,
In search of the shining day.

Thou art not with the frozen dead
Whom earth in the earth we lay,
While the bearers softly tread,
And the mourners kneel and pray;
From thy semblance, dumb and stark,
The soul has taken its flight—
Out of the finite dark,
Into the Infinite Light.

> —*Louise Chandler Moulton (1835–1908)*

In This Short Life

In this short life
That only lasts an hour,
How much, how little,
Is within our power!

> —*Emily Dickinson (1830–1886)*

Ithaka

Always keep Ithaka fixed in your mind.
To arrive there is your ultimate goal.
But do not hurry the voyage at all.
It is better to let it last for long years;
And even to anchor at the island when you are old,
Rich with all that you have gained on the way,
Not expecting that Ithaka will offer you riches.

> —*Constantine P. Cavafy (1863–1933). Read by Maurice
> Tempelsman at the 1994 funeral of Jacqueline Kennedy
> Onassis.*

A Little Work

A little work, a little play,
To keep us going—and so, good day!
A little warmth, a little light,
Of love's bestowing—and so, good night!
A little fun, to match the sorrow
Of each day's growing—and so, good morrow!
A little trust that when we die
We reap our sowing! And so—good-bye!

> —*George Louis P.B. DuMaurier (1834–1896)*

Miss Me—But Let Me Go

When I come to the end of the road
And the sun has set for me,
I want no rites in a gloom filled room!
Why cry for a soul set free!
Miss me a little—but not for long
And not with your head bowed low,
Remember the love that we once shared,
Miss me—but let me go.
For this is a journey we all must take
And each must go alone;
It's all a part of the master's plan
A step on the road to home.

When you are lonely and sick of heart
Go to the friends we know
And bury your sorrows in doing good deeds.
Miss me—but let me go.

—Edgar Albert Guest (1881–1959)

No Coward Soul

No coward soul is mine,
No trembler in the world's storm-troubled sphere:
I see Heaven's glories shine,
And Faith shines equal, arming me from Fear.

God within my breast,
Almighty, ever-present Deity!
Life, that in me has rest
As I, undying Life, have power in thee!

Vain are the thousand creeds
That move men's hearts, unutterably vain;
Worthless as withered weeds,
Or idlest froth amid the boundless main,

To wake doubt in one,
Holding so fast by thy infinity,
So surely anchored on
The steadfast rock of Immortality.

With wide-embracing love
Thy Spirit animates eternal years,
Pervades and broods above,
Changes, sustains, dissolves, creates and rears.

Though earth and man were gone,
And suns and universes ceased to be,
And Thou were left alone,
Every Existence would exit in Thee.

There is not room for Death,
Nor atom that His might could render void:
Since Thou art Being and Breath,
And what Thou art may never be destroyed.

> —*Emily Brontë (1818–1848). Read at the 1885 funeral of
> poet Emily Dickinson.*

Pleas

For all who have fully shared a love

Don't grieve too long,
once I have died, with full term spent.
As full a life there was, well shared.
For shed tears must be for yourself.
To compensate your loneliness,
without the things that once were ours.

Best dwell upon our granted time,
that we were blessed since early youth.
Of happy things. Of weathered trials.
With strength we drew from constant love.

If then you still feel incomplete.
Recall the same sun shines each day.
Don't waste it on things prior it set.
Enjoy fresh warmth that it now yields.

Keep treasured balance of fairness.
Your loneliness from other folk.
Preserving equilibrium.
To not impair remaining years.

Retain this thought: I'll not be sad.
Because you made my life complete.
Better I leave, than have to live,
the trial's of longevity.

> —*Leslie Fine (1925–)*

Reading from Henry Scott Holland (1847–1918)
Canon of St. Paul's Cathedral

Death is nothing at all, I have only slipped away into the next
    door room,
I am I and you are you...
Whatever we were to each other, that we are still.
Call me by my old familiar name, speak to me in the usual way which
    you always used.
Put no difference into your tone, wear no forced air of solemnity or
    sorrows.
Laugh as we always laughed at the little jokes we enjoyed together.
Play, smile, think of me, pray for me.
Let my name be ever the household word that it always was.
Let it be spoken without effect, without the ghost of a shadow on it.
Life means all it ever meant, it is the same as it ever was, there is
    absolutely unbroken continuity.
Why should I be out of mind, because I am out of sight?
I am but waiting for you, for in the interval. Somewhere very near just
    around the corner...All is well.

    —Author Unknown

A Reason for Life

Oft in the midst of this day's strife
I pause to wonder why
Those who living loved so well
In the dawn of life should die.

Death often makes a rendezvous
Untimely though it seems
With those who seem to have the most—
The Love of life, the dreams.
Like others from our lives they go,
But have they died in vain
Will what they gave be futile spent
To be required again?

My faith is for every loss,
Each heartache, tear and pain,
A reason, though not now discerned,
Was meant for future gain.

> —*Shelby M. Forrest (1923–)*

Song of the River

The snow melts on the mountain
And the water runs down to the spring,
And the spring in a turbulent fountain,
With a song of youth sing,
Runs down to the riotous river,
And the river flows to the sea,
And the water again
Goes back in rain
To the hills where it used to be.

And I wonder if life's deep mystery
Isn't much like the rain and the snow
Returning through all eternity
To the places it used to know.
For life was born on the lofty heights
And flows in a laughing stream,
To the river below
Whose onward flow
Ends in a peaceful dream.

And so at last,
When our life has passed
And the river has run its course,
It again goes back,
O'er the selfsame track,
To the mountain which was its source.

So why prize life
Or why fear death,
Or dread what is to be?
The river ran
Its allotted span
Till it reached the silent sea.

Then the water harked back
To the mountain-top
To begin its course once more.
So we shall run
The course begun
Till we reach the silent shore.

Then revisit earth
In a pure rebirth
From the heart of the virgin snow,
So don't ask why
We live or die,
Or whither, or when we go,
Or wonder about the mysteries
That only God may know.

—William Randolph Hearst (1863–1951)

Swiftly Beyond Our Measure

Swiftly beyond our measure
Life's little day speeds on
A moment's fleeting pleasure
And life and light are gone.
Oh thou who in human fashion,
Didst render up thy breath,
And by the bitter passion
Destroy the sting of death.
When life's brief day is over,
Its toil and care and sin
Open thine arms of mercy,
And take the weary in.

—Author Unknown

There Is No Death

There is a plan far greater than the plan you know;
There is a landscape broader than the one you see.
There is a haven where storm-tossed souls may go—

You call it death—we, immortality.
You call it death—this seeming endless sleep;
We call it birth—the soul at last set free.
'Tis hampered not by time or space—you weep.
Why weep at death? 'Tis immortality.

Farewell, dear voyageur – 'twill not be long.
Your work is done—now may peace rest with thee.
Your kindly thoughts and deeds—they will live on.
This is not death—'tis immortality.

Farewell, dear voyageur—the river winds and turns;
The cadence of your song wafts near to me,
And now you know the thing that all men learn:
There is no death—there's immortality.

> *—Author Unknown*

They Are Not Long

They are not long, the weeping and the laughter,
Love and desire and hate;
I think they have no portion in us after
We pass the gate.
They are not long, the days of wine and roses:
Out of a misty dream
Our path emerges for a while, then closes
Within a dream.

> *—Ernest Dowson (1867–1900)*

Tichborne's Elegy

My prime of youth is but a frost of cares,
My feast of joy is but a dish of pain,
My crop of corn is but a field of tares,
And all my good is but vain hope of gain;
The day is past, and yet I saw no sun,
And now I live, and now my life is done.

My tale was heard and yet it was not told,
My fruit is fallen, and yet my leaves are green,
My youth is spent and yet I am not old,

I saw the world and yet I was not seen;
My thread is cut and yet it is not spun,
And now I live, and now my life is done.

I sought my death and found it in my womb,
I looked for life and saw it was a shade,
I trod the earth and knew it was my tomb,
And now I die, and now I was but made;
My glass is full, and now my glass is run,
And now I live, and now my life is done.

—Chidiock Tichborn (1567–1586)

To a Seaman Dead on Land

Bitten to dust are the savage feathers of fire,
And the foam lies in rusted chains on the sand.
The black weeds of the sea and the conch's spire
Are brittle as bird-claws upon my hand.

My ear on the drum of the dune is hollow
Under the sabres of clanging grass—
Stark for the thunder of sails to follow,
And the throb of wings when the dark gulls pass.

Ah, but the land has silenced you,
Your blood thinning down in dew on an inland plain.
Ah, but the loud sea would have rended you
On coral stalks and the straight white horns of rain.

The sea would have pierced you with the salt of its pace,
Boomed down your sails and the ribs of your bark on stones,
Given me touch of you in the bitter foam on my face
And the sea-mist coiled like silk about your bones.

—Kay Boyle (1903–)

To Night

Mysterious Night! When our first parent knew
Thee from report divine, and heard thy name,
Did he not tremble for this lovely frame,
This glorious canopy of light and blue?

Yet 'neath a curtain of translucent dew,
Bathed in the rays of the great setting flame,
Hesperus with the host of heaven came,
And lo! Creation widened in man's view.
Who could have thought such darkness lay concealed
Within thy beams, O sun! or who could find,
Whilst fly and leaf and insect stood revealed,
That to such countless orbs thou mad'st us blind!

Why do we then shun death with anxious strife?
If Light can thus deceive, wherefore not Life?

> —*Joseph Blanco White (1775–1841). Read at the 1935
> funeral of Oliver Wendell Holmes.*

To Those I Love

If I should ever leave you whom I love
To go along the Silent Way, grieve not.
Nor speak of me with tears, but laugh and talk
Of me as if I were beside you there.
(I'd come—I'd come, could I but find a way!
But would not tears and grief be barriers?)
And when you hear a song or see a bird
I loved, please do not let the thought of me
Be sad.....For I am loving you just as
I always have.... You were so good to me!
There are so many things I wanted still
To do—so many things to say to you...
Remember that I did not fear...It was
Just leaving you that was so hard to face....
We cannot see Beyond..... But this I know:
I loved you so—'twas heaven here with you!

> —*Isla Paschal Richardson. Recited by Clark Clifford at the
> 1986 memorial service of W. Averell Harriman, and read by
> Gregory Peck at the 1998 funeral of Frank Sinatra.*

To Virgins, to Make Much of Time

Gather ye rosebuds while ye may,
Old Time is still a-flying;
And this same flower that smiles today,
To-morrow will be dying.

The glorious lamp of heaven, the Sun,
The higher he's a-getting;
The sooner will his race be run,
And nearer he's to setting.

That age is best, which is the first,
When youth and blood are warmer;
But being spent, the worse, and worst
Times still succeed the former.

Then be not coy, but use your time,
And while ye may, go marry;
For having lost but once your prime,
You may for ever tarry.

> *—Robert Herrick (1591–1674). Recited in the 1989 film*
> Dead Poets Society.

Turn Again to Life

If I should die and leave you here a while,
Be not like others, sore undone, who keep
Long vigils by the silent dust, and weep.
For my sake—turn again to life and smile,
Nerving thy heart and trembling hand to do
Something to comfort other hearts than thine.
Complete those unfinished tasks of mine
And I, perchance, may therein comfort you.

> *—Mary Lee Hall. Read by Lady Sarah McCorquodale,*
> *eldest sister of Diana, Princess of Wales, at her funeral,*
> *September 6, 1997.*

Undo It, Take It Back

Undo it, take it back, make every day the previous one until I am returned to the day before the one that made you gone. Or set me on an airplane traveling west, crossing the date line again and again, losing this day, then that, until the day of loss still lies ahead, and you are here instead of sorrow.

—Nessa Rapoport (1953–)

When I Am Gone

When I am gone release me
Let me go, I have so many things to see and do
You mustn't tie yourself to me with tears
Be happy that we had so many beautiful years
I gave to you my love
You can only guess how much you gave me in happiness
I thank you for the love you each have shown
But now it's time I travel alone
So grieve awhile for me, if grieve you must
Then let your grief be comforted by my trust
It's only for awhile that we must part
So bless the memories within your heart
I won't be far away, for life goes on
So if you need me, call and I will come
Though you can't see or touch me, I'll be near
And if you listen within your heart you'll hear
All my love around you soft and clear
And then when you must come this way alone
I'll greet you with a smile and say
"Welcome Home."

—Author Unknown

When I Die

When I die
Give what's left of me away.
To children
And those that wait to die.

And if you need to cry,
Cry for your brother
Walking the street beside you.
And when you need me,
Put your arms
Around anyone
And give them
What you need to give me.

I want to leave you something,
Something better
Than words
Or sounds.

Look for me
In the people I've known
Or loved.
And if you cannot give me away,
At least let me live in your eyes
And not in your mind.
You can love me most
By letting
Hands touch bodies,
And by letting go
Of children
That need to be free.

Love doesn't die,
People do.
So, when all that's left of me
Is love,
Give me away.

—Author Unknown

Yes Thou Art Gone

Yes, thou art gone! and never more
Thy sunny smile shall gladden me;
But I may pass the old church door,
And pace the floor that covers thee,
May stand upon the cold, damp stone,

And think that, frozen, lies below
The lightest heart that I have known,
The kindest I shall ever know.
Yet, though I cannot see thee more,
Tis still a comfort to have seen;
And though thy transient life is o'er,
Tis sweet to think that thou hast been;
To think a soul so near divine,
Within a form, so angel fair,
United to a heart like thine,
Has gladdened once our humble sphere.

            —*Anne Brontë (1820–1849)*

APPENDIX A:
SELECTED RESOURCES

Funeral Planning

Affairs in Order: A Complete Resource Guide to Death and Dying by Patricia Anderson. New York, NY: Macmillan, 1991.

The Affordable Funeral: Going in Style, Not in Debt by Rom E. Markin. Flaming Hooker Press, 1996.

Creating Meaningful Funeral Ceremonies: A Guide for Caregivers by Alan D. Wolfelt. Fort Collins, CO: Center for Loss & Life Transition, 1994.

Creating Your Own Funeral or Memorial Service: A Workbook by Stephanie West Allen. KiteShade Publishing, 1998.

Final Celebrations: A Guide for Personal and Family Funeral Planning by Kathleen Sublette. Ventura, CA: Pathfinder Pub. of California, 1992.

The Funeral Book by William Miller, Clarence W. Miller and Pamela D. Jacobs. San Francisco, CA: R.D. Reed Publishers, 1994.

Funerals Without God: A Practical Guide to Non-Religious Funerals by Jane Wynne Willson. Buffalo, NY: Prometheus Books, 1990.

The High Cost of Dying: A Guide to Funeral Planning by Gregory W. Young. Buffalo, NY: Prometheus Books, 1994.

In Memoriam: A Practical Guide to Planning a Memorial Service by Amanda Bennett and Terence B. Foley. New York, NY: Fireside, 1997.

It's Your Choice: The Practical Guide to Planning a Funeral by Thomas Nelson. Glenview, IL: Scott Foresman, 1983.

After the Funeral

PARENTS

Coping When a Parent Dies by Janet Grosshandler and Janet Grosshandler-Smith. New York, NY: Rosen Publishing Group, 1995.

145

The Day My Father Died: Women Share Their Stories of Love, Loss, and Life by Diana Ajjan (Editor). Philadelphia, PA: Running Press, 1994.

Everything You Need to Know When a Parent Dies by Fred Bratman. New York, NY: Rosen Publishing Group, 1995.

Learning to Say Good-by: When a Child's Parent Dies by Eda J. LeShan. New York, NY: Macmillan, 1976.

Letters from Motherless Daughters: Words of Courage, Grief, and Healing by Hope Edelman (Editor). New York, NY: Delta, 1996.

The Loss That Is Forever: The Lifelong Impact of the Early Death of a Mother or Father by Maxine Harris. New York, NY: Penguin Books 1996.

A Mother Loss Workbook: Healing Exercises for Daughters by Diane Hambrook, et al. New York, NY: Harper Perennial Library, 1997.

Motherless Daughters: The Legacy of Loss by Hope Edelman. Reading, MA: Perseus Books, 1994.

On Grieving the Death of a Father by Harold Ivan Smith. Minneapolis, MN: Fortress Press, 1994.

Our Mothers' Spirits: On the Death of Mothers and the Grief of Men: An Anthology by Bob Blauner (Editor). New York, NY: HarperCollins, 1998.

Recovering from the Loss of a Parent by Katherine Fair Donnelly. New York, NY: Dodd, Mead, 1987.

When Your Parent Dies: A Concise and Practical Source of Help and Advice for Adults Grieving the Death of a Parent by Cathleen L. Curry. Notre Dame, IN: Ave Maria Press, 1993.

CHILDREN

After the Darkest Hour the Sun Will Shine Again: A Parent's Guide to Coping with the Loss of a Child by Elizabeth Mehren. New York, NY: Fireside, 1997.

After the Death of a Child: Living with Loss Through the Years by Ann K. Finkbeiner. New York, NY: Free Press, 1996.

Always Precious in Our Memory: Reflections After Miscarriage, Stillbirth or Neonatal Death by Kristen J. Ingram. Chicago, IL: Acta Publications, 1997.

The Bereaved Parent by Harriet Sarnoff Schiff. New York, NY: Viking Press (Reprint edition), 1978.

The Bereaved Parents' Survival Guide by Juliet Cassuto Rothman. New York, NY: Continuum Publishing Group, 1997.

The Death of an Adult Child: A Book for and About Bereaved Parents by Jeanne Webster Blank. Amityville, NY: Baywood Publishing Company, 1997.

Empty Arms: Coping After Miscarriage, Stillbirth, and Infant Death by Sherokee Ilse. Long Lake, MN: Wintergreen Press, 1990.

Empty Cradle, Broken Heart: Surviving the Death of Your Baby by Deborah L. Davis. Golden, CO: Fulcrum Pub., 1991.

Ended Beginnings: Healing Childbearing Losses by Claudia Panuthos and Catherine Romeo. South Hadley, MA: Bergin & Garvey Publishers, 1984.

I'll Hold You in Heaven: Healings and Hope for the Parent of a Miscarried, Stillbirth Abortion or Early Infant Death by Jack Hayford. Ventura, CA: Regal Books, 1990.

How to Survive the Loss of a Child: Filling the Emptiness and Rebuilding Your Life by Catherine M. Sander. Rocklin, CA: Prima Publishing, 1998.

Miscarriage: A Shattered Dream by Sherokee Ilse and Linda Hammer Burns. Wintergreen Press (Reissue edition), 1992.

Miscarriage: Women Sharing from the Heart by Marie Allen and Shelly Marks. New York, NY: John Wiley & Sons, 1993.

Our Stories of Miscarriage: Healing with Words by Rachel Faldet and Karen Fitton, editors. Minneapolis, MN: Fairview Press, 1997.

Recovering from the Loss of a Child by Katherine Fair Donnelly. New York, NY: Macmillan, 1982.

Surviving Pregnancy Loss: A Complete Sourcebook for Women and Their Families by Rochelle Friedman and Bonnie Gradstein. Secaucus, NJ: Carol Pub. Group, 1996.

The Ultimate Loss: Coping with the Death of a Child by Joan Bordow. New York, NY: Beaufort Books, 1982.

The Worst Loss: How Families Heal from the Death of a Child by Barbara D. Rosof. New York, NY: Henry Holt and Company, 1994.

Soul Mates, Spouses and Lovers

After Goodbye: How to Begin Again After the Death of Someone You Love by Theodore Menten. Philadelphia, PA: Running Press, 1994.

Beginnings: A Book for Widows by Betty Jane Wylie and Jonathan Webb. Fourth Revised Edition. Toronto, Ontario: McClelland & Stewart, 1997.

Being a Widow by Lynn Caine. New York, NY: Penguin USA, 1990.

Beyond Widowhood: From Bereavement to Emergence and Hope by Robert DiGuilio. New York, NY: Free Press, 1989.

Companion to Grief: Finding Consolation When Someone You Love Has Died by Patricia Kelley. New York, NY: Simon & Schuster, 1997.

The Death of a Wife: Reflections for a Grieving Husband by Robert L. Vogt. Chicago, IL: Acta Publications, 1997.

How to Go on Living When Someone You Love Dies by Therese A. Rando. New York, NY: Bantam Books, 1991.

How to Survive the Loss of a Love by Melba Colgrove. Los Angeles, CA: Prelude Press, 1993.

Living Again: A Personal Journey for Surviving the Loss of a Spouse by William Wallace. Lenexa, KS: Addax Publishing Group, 1998.

A Time to Grieve: Meditations for Healing After the Death of a Loved One by Carol Staudacher. San Francisco, CA: Harper, 1994.

When Your Spouse Dies: A Concise and Practical Source of Help and Advice by Cathleen L. Curry. Notre Dame, IN: Ave Maria Press, 1990.

Widowed by Dr. Joyce Brothers. New York, NY: Simon & Schuster, 1990.

Widower: When Men Are Left Alone by Phyllis R. Silverman and Scott D. Campbell. Amityville, NY: Baywood Publishing Company, 1996.

FRIENDS

Grieving the Death of a Friend by Harold Ivan Smith. Minneapolis, MN: Augsburg Fortress Pub, 1996.

Letters to a Dying Friend: Helping Those You Love Make a Conscious Transition by Kern Foundation. Wheaton, IL: Quest Books (Revised edition), 1997.

When a Friend Dies: A Book for Teens About Grieving & Healing by Marilyn E. Gootman. Minneapolis, MN: Free Spirit Pub, 1994.

SIBLINGS

For Those Who Live: Helping Children Cope with the Death of a Brother or Sister by Kathy Latour. Omaha, NE: Centering Corp (Revised edition), 1987.

Losing Someone You Love: When a Brother or Sister Dies by Elizabeth Richter. New York, NY: Putnam, 1986.

Recovering from the Loss of a Sibling by Katherine Fair Donnelly. New York, NY: Dodd, Mead, 1988.

Sibling Loss by Joanna H. Fanos. Mahwah, NJ: Lawrence Erlbaum Associates, 1996.

Unspoken Grief: Coping with Childhood Sibling Loss by Helen Rosen. Lexington, MA: Lexington Books, 1986.

COMPANION ANIMALS

Coping with Sorrow on the Loss of Your Pet by Moira K. Anderson. Loveland, CO: Alpine Pubns (Second edition), 1996.

The Final Farewell; Preparing for and Mourning the Loss of Your Pet by Marty Tousley and Katherine Heuerman. Our Pals Publishing Company, 1997.

For the Love of Princess: Surviving the Loss of Your Pet by Cheryl A. Kilbourn. Princess Pub, 1987.

Goodbye, Dear Friend: Coming to Terms with the Death of a Pet by Virginia Ironside. New York, NY: Robson Books/Parkwest, 1997.

Goodbye, Friend: Healing Wisdom for Anyone Who Has Ever Lost a Pet by Gary Kowalski. Walpole, NH: Stillpoint Pub, 1997.

Healing the Pain of Pet Loss: Letters in Memoriam by Kymberly Smith (Editor). Philadelphia, PA: Charles Press, 1997.

The Heart That Is Loved Never Forgets: Recovering from Loss: When Humans and Animals Lose Their Companions by Kaetheryn Walker. Rochester, VT: Healing Arts Press, 1998.

It's Okay to Cry by Maria L. Quintana, et al. Perrysburg, OH: K & K Communications, 1998.

The Loss of a Pet by Wallace Sife. New York, NY: Howell Books Inc, 1993.

Loving and Losing a Pet: A Psychologist and a Veterinarian Share Their Wisdom by Michael Stern and Susan Cropper. Northvale, NJ: Jason Aronson, 1998.

Pet Loss: A Spiritual Guide by Eleanor L. Harris. St. Paul, MN: Llewellyn, 1997.

Pet Loss: A Thoughtful Guide for Adults & Children by Herbert A. Nieburg, et al. New York, NY: Harper Perennial (Reprint edition), 1996.

A Special Place for Charlee: A Child's Companion Through Pet Loss by Debby Morehead. Broomfield, CO: Partners in Publishing, 1996.

Surviving the Heartbreak of Choosing Death for Your Pet by Linda Mary Peterson. Tempe, AZ: Greentree Pub, 1997.

When Your Pet Dies by Christine Adamec. New York, NY: Berkley Pub Group, 1996.

GRIEF AND BEREAVEMENT

Afterloss: A Recovery Companion for Those Who Are Grieving by Barbara Hills Lesstrang. Nashville, TN: T. Nelson, 1992.

After You Say Goodbye: When Someone You Love Dies of AIDS by Paul Kent Froman. San Francisco, CA: Chronicle Books, 1992.

As Someone Dies: A Handbook for the Living by Elizabeth A. Johnson. Carlsbad, CA: Hay House (Revised edition), 1995.

Coping with Bereavement by Hamish McIlwraith. Rockport, MA: Element, 1998.

Courage to Grieve by Judy Tatelbaum. New York, NY: Lippincott & Crowell, 1980.

Finding My Way: Healing and Transformation Through Loss and Grief by John M. Schneider. Colfax, Wis: Seasons Press, 1994.

Good Grief: A Constructive Approach to the Problem of Loss by Granger E. Westberg. Minneapolis, MN: Fortress Press, 1986.

Giving Sorrow Words: How to Cope with Grief and Get on with Your Life by Candy Lightner. New York, NY: Warner Books, 1990.

The Grief Recovery Handbook: The Action Program for Moving Beyond Death, Divorce, and Other Losses by John W. James and Russell Friedman. New York, NY: HarperCollins (Revised edition), 1998.

Healing After the Suicide of a Loved One by Ann Smolin, et al. New York, NY: Fireside, 1993.

The Mourning Handbook: A Complete Guide for the Bereaved by Helen Fitzgerald. New York, NY: Simon & Schuster, 1994.

My Companion Through Grief: Comfort for Your Darkest Hours by Gary Kinnaman. Ann Arbor, MI: Servant Publications, 1996.

No Time to Say Goodbye: Surviving the Suicide of a Loved One by Carla Fine. New York, NY: Doubleday, 1997.

Silent Grief: Living in the Wake of Suicide by Christopher Lukas and Henry M. Seiden Northvale, NJ: Jason Aronson, 1997.

A Woman's Book of Grieving by Nessa Rapaport. New York, NY: William Morrow, 1994.

APPENDIX B:
SELECTED SUPPORT
ORGANIZATIONS

A.M.E.N.D.
(Aiding a Mother and Father Experiencing Neonatal Death)
Provides support to parents who have experienced the loss of an infant through miscarriage, stillbirth or neonatal death.

    1559 Ville Rosa
    Hazelwood, MO 63042
    Phone: (314) 291-0892

American Association of Suicidology
http://www.users.interport.net/-lindy/aas.html
Attempts to understand and prevent suicide, promote research, public awareness programs, and educate and train professionals and volunteers. Serves as a national clearinghouse on information about suicide.

    4201 Connecticut Ave, NW, Suite 310
    Washington, DC 20008
    Phone: (202) 237-2280
    Fax: (202) 237-2282

American Self-Help Clearinghouse
http://www.cmhc.com/selfhelp/
Provides information on local self-help groups worldwide to assist people in finding or forming bereavement self-help support groups.

    Northwest Covenant Medical Center
    Denville, New Jersey 07834-2995
    Phone: (201) 625-9565
    Fax: (201) 625-8848
    Email: asch@buttercup.cybernex.net

Association for Death Education and Counseling
http://www.adec.org
Provides death education and death-related counseling by conducting work-shops, distributing educational materials and certifying death educators.
  638 Prospect Avenue
  Hartford, Connecticut 06105-4298
  Phone: (860) 586-7503
  Fax: (860) 586-7550
  Email: sserpa@aol.com

Bereavement and Hospice Support Netline
http://ube.ubalt.edu/www/bereavement/
An online directory of bereavement and hospice support groups and services.

Bereavement Services
Provides referrals based on the individual needs of parents who have experi-enced miscarriage, ectopic pregnancy, stillbirth or newborn deaths.
  Gundersen Lutheran Medical Center
  1910 South Avenue
  LaCrosse, WI 54601
  Phone: (800) 362-9567
  Fax: (608) 791-5137
  Email: berservs@LHL.6undluth.org

The Compassionate Friends
Assists bereaved parents and siblings with the grief experienced upon the death of a child.
  P.O. Box 3696
  Oak Brook, Illinois 60522-3696
  Phone: (708) 990-0010
  Fax: (708) 990-0246

The Dougy Center for Grieving Children
Provides support for children grieving a death.
  3903 S.E. 52nd Avenue
  P.O. Box 86582
  Portland, Oregon 97286
  Phone: (503) 775-5683

GriefNet
http://rivendell.org
An Internet resource that can connect the user with a variety of resources related to death, dying, bereavement, and major emotional and physical losses.
  Rivendell Resources
  P.O. Box 3272
  Ann Arbor, Michigan 48106-3272
  Email: rivendel@falcon.ic.net

Heartbeat
Provides support and direction for people who have lost a loved one to suicide.
2015 Devon Street
Colorado Springs, CO 80909
Phone: (719) 596-2575

Hospice Foundation of America
http://www.hospicefoundation.org
Provides information and education about the care of terminally ill people.
Suite 300, 2001 S Street NW
Washington, DC 20009
Phone: (202) 638-5312 / (800) 854-3402
Fax: (202) 638-5312
Email: hospicefdn@charitiesusa.com

In Loving Memory
A support organization dedicated to helping parents cope with the death of their
only child or all of their children.
1416 Green Run Lake
Reston, Virginia 22090
Phone: (703) 435-0608

International THEOS Foundation
A support network for recently widowed men and women that sponsors pro-
grams and provide services to help participants work through their immediate
grief and cope with day-to-day practical concerns of widowhood.
322 Boulevard of the Allies, Suite 105
Pittsburgh, PA 15222-1919
Phone: (412) 471-7779
Fax: (412) 471-7782

Miscarriage, Infant Death, Stillbirth Support Group
Offers support to parents who have experienced the loss of an infant.
c/o Janet Tischler
16 Crescent Drive
Parsippany, NJ 07054-1605
Phone: (201) 263-6730

The National Funeral Directors Association
http://www.nfda.org
Produces educational materials including books, brochures, and audiovisuals
on dying, death, funeral customs and bereavement for both funeral directors
and consumers.
11121 West Oklahoma Avenue/ PO Box 27641
Milwaukee, Wisconsin 53227-0641
Phone: (414) 541-2500
Fax: (414) 541-1909

National Organization of Parents of Murdered Children
Provides support to help parents and other survivors deal with the pain of their loss and facilitate the reconstruction of their lives.
>   100 East Street, B-41
>   Cincinnati, Ohio 45202
>   Phone: (513) 721-5683

National SHARE Office (Pregnancy and Infant Loss Support, Inc.)
http://www.NationalSHAREOffice.com
Provides support for people troubled by the death of a baby through miscarriage, stillbirth, or newborn death.
>   St. Joseph Health Center
>   300 First Capitol Drive
>   St. Charles, Missouri 63301-2893
>   Phone: (800) 821-6819
>   Fax: (314) 947-7486

Pet Loss Partnership
http://www.vetmed.wsu.edu/ppp.html
Provides support for grieving people who have experienced pet loss.
>   College of Veterinary Medicine
>   Washington State University
>   Pullman, Washington 99164-7010
>   Phone: (509) 335-4569

Pregnancy and Infant Loss Center
Provides information, referral, comfort, understanding, resources, and perspective to individuals and families who have experienced the death of their baby.
>   1421 East Wayzata Boulevard, Suite #30
>   Wayzata, Minnesota 55391
>   Phone: (612) 473-9372
>   Fax: (612) 473-8978

Rainbows
Assists in the establishment of peer support groups for children, adolescents, and adults who are grieving a death, divorce, or other painful transition in their family.
>   1111 Tower Road
>   Schaumburg, Illinois 60173-4305
>   Phone: (800 266-3206
>   Fax: (847) 310-0120
>   Email: rainbowshdqtrs@worldnet.att.net

Ray of Hope, Inc.
A national self-help organization for coping with suicide, loss, and grief.
P.O. Box 2323
Iowa City, Iowa 52244
Phone: (319) 337-9890

Society of Military Widows
Provides support to women whose husbands died on active duty military service or during retirement from the armed forces.
5535 Hempstead Way
Springfield, VA 22151
Phone: (703) 750-1342 X3007
Fax: (703) 354-4380
Email: mconaus@aol.com

Sudden Infant Death Syndrome (SIDS) Alliance
Dedicated to eliminating SIDS through research, serving SIDS families, education professionals and the general public about SIDS.
1314 Bedford Avenue, Suite 210
Baltimore, Maryland 21208
Phone: (410) 653-8826 / (800) 221-SIDS
Fax: (410) 659-8709

Unite, Inc.
Provides grief support following the death of a baby, including miscarriage, ectopic pregnancy, stillbirth, and infant death.
7600 Central Avenue
Philadelphia, PA 19111-2499
Phone: (215) 728-3777

CREDITS

A.E. Housman, "To an Athlete Dying Young" from *The Collected Poems of A.E. Housman,* Copyright 1939, 1940, © 1965 by Henry Holt and Company, Inc. 1967, 1968 by Robert E. Symons.

"I Only Wanted You" from The Pet Loss Grief Support Website & Candle Ceremony Internet WWW page, at URL: <http://www.petloss.com/onlyyou. htm> (version current at 4 October 1998).

David Ignatow, "Kaddish." Copyright © 1980 by David Ignatow. Reprinted by permission of Yaedi Ignatow, literary executor. "Vanishment (for Rose)." Copyright © 1997 by David Ignatow. Reprinted by permission of Yaedi Ignatow, literary executor.

Yaedi Ignatow, "Lives, Like Mercury (for Ted Jacqueney)." Copyright © 1998 by Yaedi Ignatow. Reprinted by permission of the author.

Elizabeth Jennings, "The Unknown Child," from *Collected Poems.* Manchester: Carcanet Press Limited. Reprinted by permission of David Higham Associates Limited.

Rudyard Kipling, "The Power of the Dog" from *Dogs in the Writings of Rudyard Kipling.* Centreville, VA: Denlingers Publishers, Ltd., 1991. Copyright © 1991 by Denlingers Publishers, Ltd. Reprinted by permission of the publisher.

Denise Levertov, "At David's Grave" from poems 1968–1972. Copyright © 1970 by Denise Levertov. Reprinted by permission of New Directories Publishing Corp.

Jack Link, "Give What's Left of Me Away" from The People Against Cancer Internet WWW page, at URL:<http://main.dodgenet.com/ nocancer/optionstxt495.html> (version current at 4 October 1998).

Audre Lorde, "If You Come Softly" from *Collected Poems.* Copyright © 1968 by Audre Lorde. Reprinted by permission of W.W. Norton & Company, Inc.

John Gillespie Magee, Jr., "High Flight" from *Poetry of the World Wars.* London: Michael O'Mara Books Ltd, 1990. Copyright © 1990 by Michael O'Mara Books Ltd.

Leo Marks, "Code Poem for the French Resistance" from Radio Collection BBC/The Nation's Favourite Love Poems—Disc 1 Internet WWW page, at URL:<http://www.cddb.com/xm/cd/misc/85115729.html> (version current at 4 October 1998).

FILM, NOVEL AND FAMOUS PERSON INDEX

TITLE AND FIRST LINE INDEX

AUTHOR INDEX